MINISTRY
OF MISDEMEANOUR

Sequel to *The Boy with Shoes*

A Memoir

HILLARY LISIMBA AMBANI

MYSTERY PUBLISHERS
Redefining African Stories

MYSTERY BOOKS
Ministry of Misdemeanour

Kindle Edition by Mystery Books, an Imprint of Mystery Publishers — 2020
Smashwords Edition by Mystery Books — 2020

This Paperback Edition:

ISBN-13: 978-9966-955-16-6

Published by:
Mystery Publishers Limited
P.O. Box 18016 – Nakuru, Kenya
Tel: +254 718 429 184
Email: publishing@mysterypublisherslimited.com
Website: www.mysterypublisherslimited.com

Cover Design by Vincent de Paul ©Mystery Books
Cover illustration by Abel Murumba ©Mystery Books
Typeset in Minion Pro 12pt by Mystery Publishers

Printed in Kenya by:
Core Media
P.O. Box 47433—00100
Nairobi, Kenya
Email: info@coremedia.co.ke

Available from Mystery Bookstore, Amazon, Kindle and other online retailers.

For my late Dad

A gallant life soldier whose shoes I was left to fill.

I write to you, not that it makes sense to, but because you feature in this book, albeit posthumously. I started writing it when you were still part of us, but then it was yet to hit home that sometimes people depart like candle flames in the ranging winds. You are not here to read, but the young man named after you is doing a great job at keeping the brand alive. He has your fighting spirit, that same one I witnessed as you fought tooth and nail to remain in the land of the living. You were overpowered, but I was proud of you, and I know you slipped away with your head held high. In times of war, fathers bury their sons, they say, and in times of peace, sons bury their fathers. I guess that is to say we lost you in peace. May it prevail.

From your Son, with a Salute;

*Dedicated to all those whose teenage mistakes inscribed
an indelible mark on their lives, forever.*

CONTENTS

PREFACE

THERE IS HIGH SCHOOL, AND then there is HIGH SCHOOL. The first is tamed and packaged with all the wonderful adjectives that society can relate to well-educated youth. The latter, is chaotic. It is shrouded in hooliganism and self-discovery that turn boys into men, and girls into women. This sort of high school delivers street smartness, a lesson no book offers. The first creates and streamlines its subjects into the dos and don'ts of life. For instance, do not disrespect authority. The second type molds; thus, allowing the curious minds an opportunity to answer the question of 'what if?' What if I disrespect the said authority? What if I have unprotected sex? What if I break rules?

High school lives in the present, constantly pumping formulas and methods into its constituents. However, some may never come in the final examination, or help them once they exit the gate after completing their final year exams. On the other hand, HIGH SCHOOL lives in the future. It imparts skills and experience on how to maneuver through life in the world outside school. High school instills fear in students; constantly subjecting them to psychological torture over poor grades, and how performing poorly equals a bad future. HIGH SCHOOL inculcates bravery. This makes students realize that mistakes can be made, and rectified without locking out potential opportunities.

High school is like a spherical globe in an astronomy lab. It revolves depending on the direction you push it, and a new part of the world comes into view, while another is thrust out of view. The days and nights as well as seasons of wealth, poverty, and stagnation are components that form the globe. Those who are quick enough to understand the secret, spin it in the right direction. Thus, they create a stable foundation to hinge their life just like the epic third little pig, who built his house using stone. High school is also like the vast sea, where all you see when you look at the blue water is calmness, but underneath is a behemoth of vicious waves that swallow mammoth vessels into oblivion. The trick is studying the tide, and knowing when and where to set sail, that way you glide over smoothly, on a good day aided by the wind.

You must by now be wondering which of the two I went to. HIGH SCHOOL is where I attended and learnt three important things; how to survive cash flow challenges, entrepreneurship, and the responsibility that comes with freedom. None of those were examined in the four years, but they have come in handy decades later. However, there was a flipside that sculpted most of us from naïve and scared villagers into goons. As too daring people, we scrapped through to the end. When we were caught somewhere between boys and men, the grey areas opened our eyes to a world of discovery and tempting fate. The more heinous crimes one committed without being discovered, the greater the accolades. Whereas parents and teachers called it high school, I summed it up as a giant *Ministry of Misdemeanor.*

What I present here is a true recollection as and when things happened. People, events, names and places have, however, been altered mildly or greatly to protect identities, families, and loved ones.

PROLOGUE

THOSE DAYS, THE MINISTRY OF Education released the final primary school results a few days to the New Year. The names of the best performers were splashed all over mainstream media. Names of those who failed to meet the minimum threshold were mentioned in hushed tones and viewed as the black sheep. In a country with not only a crippled public education system, but also fewer spaces in institutions of higher learning, this tradition created motion and emotion among thousands of students and parents countrywide. There was motion for those who performed well, as they started putting in place measures to transition into the next phase of their education. Emotion filled for those who tripped as they dithered on whether to retake the class the following year, take up vocational training, or call it a day on their education journey.

The embarrassment of repeating class eight knocked out many from that option, and chances at vocational training centres were limited. Sometimes, these positions were bought, which left many with the last option—dropping out. Girls were married off, their parents hoping to salvage a buck off dowry lest the idleness in the villages that brought forth unwanted babies. It was bad to get pregnant while in your parents' home, that earned you the title 'damaged goods'. Boys joined the *bodaboda* industry, overloading pillions on leased motorbikes for a few coins that ended up in illicit brew dens. The lucky few who possessed innate entrepreneurial skills pooled together a bit of financing, invested in businesses and rebuilt their would-be messed lives from ground up, after rectifying childhood mistakes to live a decent life.

Then there was us, who luckily or forcibly, managed to rake in the marks that guaranteed a chance in not just any secondary school, but a well performing one; provincial or national. So, when my letter came and I had been offered a chance at Akili High School, my parents were elated. I was too, especially after years of being the most hated student in my primary school for having shoes when everyone else walked barefooted.

FINDING THE HAYSTACK

A YOUNG MAN WITH A beaming smile approached me. He introduced himself as the captain to Kilimanjaro, the dormitory I had been allocated. He was accompanied by a shorter man, with bushy hair and big round eyes, who told me to call him Phillo.

"Mono!" they called me.

"My name is Hillary," I countered.

They looked at each other, grinned mischievously, and quipped, "Mono, get up and go to the dormitory."

Two other boys joined us. Although they seemed to be accomplices, the new pair did not introduce themselves. I was hardly half a day old in the goddamned school and I was already annoyed. The four young men carried away my belongings—one picking the basin, and another my mattress, while two carried my locked metal box.

"Bro, Monos in this school are just there to be seen, not heard," Phillo announced as I followed the quartet, like a ram.

Kilimanjaro was an old rectangular structure burrowed between two dormitories; New Kenya to the right and Elgon to the left. Each structure was surrounded by flower beds serving as boundaries to demarcate where each territory extended to, with a stretch of no-man's land in between. A medium-sized tree with no fruits stood at the entrance; it was too surrounded by a round flower bed that appeared to have been weeded a few days ago. The name 'KILIMANJARO' written in cursive above the door was faint, devastated by decades of dust, cobwebs and other weather elements. The corrugated iron sheets contended with the hideous dark brown colour; mnemonic of how colossal amounts of corrosion had worn it down. Where the glass window panes once filled in for many years, there were gaping spaces letting in flushes of cold February air ingested by the tens of miserable haphazard beds.

"Welcome to our *palace*," my hosts told me. "Fit in as fast as possible."

The 'palace' was an assembly of two double-decker beds facing each other, with a space between the beds for movement. It was nothing close to magnificent golden chairs, and puffed up men in red satin outfits guarding a royal. You cannot even begin naming somewhere a palace, when it had a malodorous stench of unwashed socks hanging in the air. Between setting up my newly allocated bed on the upper deck, and learning that I would now be called a pilot, my *trough* (basin) and bag of snacks that Thatcher packed for me that morning had disappeared with the two boys who had refused to introduce themselves earlier. It was like voodoo; now you see them, now you don't. When I tried to inquire from the remaining two, I was reminded how Monos within that compound are only seen, but not heard.

As quickly as my hosts had picked and dumped me in the dormitory, they disappeared for their afternoon lessons, leaving me to wallow in thoughts and loneliness. I was surrounded by empty beds, hurriedly spread in faded blue sheets and pairs of dirty socks hanging on the headboards. I had my pair of socks, only that my two pairs were new. They still carried that scent of new fabric from the emporium. There was no single bed with a mosquito net, and I knew too well that it was not on the list of things I had carried from home that morning. *Mosquitoes must have had field days in this part of the world.* The sad bit was that I was the latest addition to the growing list of humans for them to prey on. I wondered just how much this place froze during the cold season seeing there were no window panes.

I looked at my bed, fresh and neatly made with new sheets; a complete juxtaposition of the rest. The beds were too small for the grown men I had seen bullying their way into the dining hall. The mattresses on the beds were decrepit. Most had huge chunks of the sponge missing like a loaf of bread whose spongy interior had been eaten away. It was as if people pinched and ate mattresses in this dormitory, but it was expected if those malnourished people I had seen scuttle towards the dining hall was anything to go by.

To kill boredom, I practised tying a tie the way Dad had taught me the previous weekend. We had spent minutes going through the steps until I was a pro. He did a good job on that one; what I could not comprehend was why the inventor of the tie complicated the process.

My stomach grumbled, reminding me that I had only taken breakfast that morning. It intensified when I remembered that my snacks had gone missing like a plume of smoke in the wind. There was some pocket money in my wallet, but where was the school canteen? I counted the money again—three hundred shillings. Mom had taken the trouble of giving it in coins of five, ten and twenty to help me have 'loose' cash for easier transactions. It looked like a lot of money. She had proposed I hand it to the school bursar for safekeeping, but I decided to ignore her advice. My coins will remain with me, if I die in this damned place, I die with them. Why allow her to continue micromanaging me? I was a big boy now, *babba*, time to leave the geckos and swim with the crocodiles.

Joining boarding school could not have come at a better time for Mom since she would get reprieve from my shenanigans, after many years of shouting herself hoarse. On my part, it was time and freedom to experience life on my own. Another year of being in each other's faces would have forced one of us out of Dad's compound, and the culprit would have been ME; the self-proclaimed Duke of Vihiga.

My uniform was an ensemble of navy blue trousers, navy blue pullover, black shoes, grey socks with a thin white strip across and a snow-white shirt. On the shirt pocket was the conspicuous Akili Boys' High School badge with the motto 'Education is the Light.' Mom had dragged me to an underwear boutique the previous weekend, from which I stepped out with six new pairs. We counted one to six; SIX NEW UNDERWEAR at once! I wondered whether I was going to boarding school to study or engage in underwear contests.

I was four and a half feet tall, skinny, dark, and naive,

babied by my mother since birth. Mom may have been a disciplinarian, but she never allowed us to do house chores. For a family that had started making some money after starting in squalor, my parents decided to pacify their years of toil by employing a house help, gardener, cow boy, and the occasional farm help. That essentially rendered my siblings and me little ineptitudes, whose job was to eat, poop, and sleep. I would be lying to say we were rich. My family had food, a permanent house, clothing, and school fees, but things like a family car, kids' bicycles, or house telephone were considered luxuries that existed in a side of life we were yet to reach.

Raised under a strict regime that revolved around home and school, my sisters and I were doing badly when it came to building relationships outside the permitted circle. I once brought a primary school friend home, but the eyes he was given served as a harbinger for our introversion.

So, being frog-marched to boarding school that chilly morning marked the beginning of a journey I had missed out on for over a decade. It was one of self-discovery, creating healthy attachments, and earning life skills. I was being yanked away from the comforts of getting everything on the proverbial silver platter, with several hands waiting to clean up after me. This would be replaced by me being in charge of my own health, time, and finances, never mind that I had been raised in a household where it was illegal for children to possess money.

For four years, I would call Akili High School home three terms every year, each compacted into three months with a four-week break separating them. All eyes were on signing me into boarding school that no one noticed the emotional turmoil I was battling inside. I pendulumed between the fear of the unknown and feelings of abandonment. On the contrary, there was excitement of being away from the woman I had had run-ins with, Thatcher.

Mom, known to many as Madam Jane, was a darling of the community, but a terrorist at home. She would always find the next available reason to flog me, her only begotten son, so I picked rebellious tendencies to survive. That's why I nicknamed her Thatcher, after the British Prime Minister—Margaret Thatcher—the Iron Lady.

Growing up, Thatcher would beat me for my crimes, my younger sisters' mistakes, and those I was yet to commit. To revenge, I would replace working bulbs in her room with blown up ones, throw stones over her house at night, or steal stupid things from the neighbours' farms, like pumpkins or maize cobs. The joy I derived from that was out of this world.

Earlier that day, a *matatu* dropped us on the main road and zoomed away; leaving on the ground my 2 by 4 inch mattress, blue basin, metallic box, and hockey stick. The fact that I had to carry all those items to the school uphill was my first consideration of truancy. As we trudged the rocky path with the metallic box on my head, the weight pushed the neck slowly into my torso. Oblivious that her son was only managing to walk, Thatcher blubbered beside me about how she would no longer be around to keep tabs on me. Her words were water through a sieve in my ears.

I was still looking for the perfect place to dump the metallic box, and tell Thatcher to spend what would have been my school fees on something more lucrative, when a white Toyota Chaser stopped beside me. The driver was motioning for us to move closer. Thatcher was too engrossed in her lecture to notice, so I tore away from her and went to hear what the driver was saying. A middle-aged man in glasses, a grey three-piece suit and red tie sat behind the wheel. He had all the makings of a pastor, this good Samaritan. Like a dehydrated desert ranger, who comes upon an oasis oozing fresh water, I flung my box into the trunk and hopped into the car. I breathed a heavy sigh of relief because, from my calculation, if I had carried the box on my head all the way, I would have gotten there minus a neck, like a button mushroom.

In the backseat was a young man dressed in the same uniform as mine, looking confused like myself. I wondered quietly if his mother, probably the woman seated at the front, had imposed loads of innerwear on him too.

This was a lucky boy to be chauffeur-driven to his new school. It was warm inside the car, and the man was jovial. I immediately felt at home in a car whose occupants I did not know yet.

I left the door open for Thatcher to come in, which she did with a smile. A greeting escaped her lips, but I could tell from her facial expression she hoped for an opportunity to slap me silly for 'jumping into strangers' cars contrary to her repeated warnings. We drove on in silence, a cassette of Munishi's *Malebo* playing on the car stereo. My dad once owned the same album, but I had mutilated it the day I discovered reggae and dubbed a UB40 album over that tape, a mischief that almost cost my stay in his house. He had since recovered from that heartbreak, but never replaced the album.

The dusty road leading to the school was lined with trees and flowers on both sides, each with writings on wooden planks hanging on the branches. I quickly understood that everything in this school was labelled, for whatever reason. The trees stood tall around a huge field divided into two; one side with football goalposts and another with smaller ones for hockey. Further down were little white colonial houses, and Thatcher was convinced they were teachers' quarters. Near them was parked a long blue and white bus with the school name written across its body.

When we got to the admissions office, we let the 'good Samaritans' lead on the admission queue. When you are of a lower class you easily relinquish such pleasures. It gave me the first feeling of inferiority; that I was now in an environment with boys who were chauffeured to school back-left while I walked on foot like a hound. Thatcher must have noticed the change. She slipped into inspirational mode on how boarding school is a unifying factor, since everyone leaves their backgrounds at home to share a common environment.

After the admission, I was directed to a waiting bench from which we exchanged goodbyes. I watched with a feeling of emptiness as Thatcher disappeared in the distance. Who would have thought that after years of enduring her constant haranguing, I would be the one holding back tears? My heart shattered, but I collected the pieces and put them together unlike the fellow newbie who broke down and cried until veins popped out the sides of his forehead. It was so intense that he lost his voice, leaving him wheezing. His dispirited crying earned him two sympathizers, who joined in, turning the bench into a crying party. I could not imagine the son of Ambani crying because of being left by Mother.

A bell rung, and in not so long, rangy students thronged past our bench like soldiers mounting a parade. They then disappeared behind one of the buildings. They all looked malnourished; skinny tramps with pale skin and shaggy hair. They seemed like they clung to life by an attenuate thread. I swear if something happened and they missed a meal, they would all have died. Their eyes were sunken, threatening to disappear into their sockets at the slightest provocation. Compared to how neat and chubby we, the newcomers, were, that skinny army had dirty shoes, faded trousers, brown shirts and no ties. It was like we were from two different schools. Most of their pullovers sagged at the V-necks, unlike mine that hugged my body like a mermaid's dress. Each carried a plate and spoon; an indication that I had sat there doing nothing from morning to lunch time.

Admission to high school was like looking for the proverbial needle in a haystack. The difference was that we were still too far from the needle; the plan here was to find the haystack itself, after which the search would be narrowed down.

My new home, Akili Boys' High School, was like one gigantic plantation from which hay was grown. The hay was represented by the lessons both in and out of class, forging partnerships, managing money, expressing ourselves and seeking working solutions out of difficult situations. The haystacks were in the form of dreams and ambitions, our hopes for the future, our careers, our whole lives.

I was here to find out which particular area of the plantation grew hay that would interest me, from which the needle would be sought later in the form of a job, wealth and the good life (if the analogies of hard work paying came to pass.) And by the way, I never saw my trough again for the rest of the years I spent there.

FLYING SQUAD

Hunger Took Toll Of Me. I decided to step out of the dormitory and roam around hoping to find the school canteen. A pair of keys jingled right next to my crotch. Mom had put them for me on a key holder. She insisted I latch it onto one of the belt loops on my trouser, a place I would not only access easily, but also keep watch over. In her words, 'a society with people from different walks of life is not devoid of thieves.' I hated the idea, but then her reasons for me walking with a jingling crotch made sense. There and then a new indecision popped up—whether to move around with the whole bunch, leave one set locked in the box, or take it to the bursar for safekeeping. My mind was not in the right frame to make critical decisions with the hunger, so I ambled out of the dormitory. I followed the pavement and wandered towards old structures, looking out for any signpost that could lead me to a canteen.

"Young man, come here." An imperious voice shouted from behind.

I turned to see a man in a navy blue trouser, white shirt and black shoes pointing a bamboo cane at me. His dressing was almost similar to the boys who had swindled my snacks; the only missing piece on him was the tie. He did not strike me as someone I should be afraid of; he looked like another rogue student out to take advantage of my confusion. Having learnt the hard way from the brutal welcome, and fully aware that I was here to be seen, no one else was getting it easy with me. I was officially in fight mode, coupled with hunger, agitation, and homesickness. I dawdled towards him, my blood starting to boil.

"Form One?" He inquired, gaze fixed on my crotch.

He had quickly scanned the position of my keys and figured I was a newbie. I knew this one was about to *monolize* me, but he was going to pay for the sins perpetrated by his predecessors.

"Yes, I am a Form One. Does that bother you?" I answered, throwing an impertinent eye.

His eyes roved over me from top to bottom, like a human scanner scanning a suspected drug mule at the airport.

"Where are you from, and where are you going to?" He prodded.

"I am from the dormitory and I'm out here looking for something to eat. Now would you be kind and show me the canteen instead of these unnecessary questions?"

He started walking while motioning me to follow, his demeanour friendlier this time. I walked behind him like a car being towed by a *breakdown*, a position that made me notice a dark patch behind his left ear. We finally got to the canteen. I bought one soda and a pack of biscuits.

"What's your name?"

"Hillary." I quipped, watching him walk away.

Being firm had helped me on this one, I thought. Way to go. I strolled back into loneliness, missing home . . . and Mom. I thought about my trough. Whoever snatched it did not even let me use it for a day. It was quite a rude and unpopular welcome into boarding school. It had sounded like hogwash when Mom said it as we came for admission earlier that day, but now it was clear that I was officially on my own in an unforgiving world. I started missing her patronage that I had so much wanted to break away from.

"Be careful with what you say and who you tell. Spies live among us." That was the earliest warning I received from the first chap I made friends with that evening.

Apparently, the administration had *moles* among students, who eavesdropped on conversations and forwarded the sensitive information. Moles were never known who they were. However, it was rumoured that most would be made prefects later in the year to throw the trail into disarray, then a new set was installed and everyone had to start foraging again. Nevertheless, one way to smell a mole was when the character in question subsequently tried to initiate negative conversations about the administration and solicited opinion. Those were ears picking out dissenting voices to be added on the list that would be closely monitored.

Moles also seemed to get away with felonies, so if two or more of you were caught up in some punishable offence and 'forgiven,' someone in that group was swinging the other way. Question would always be 'who?' With such doubts planted in each other, budding friendships would deteriorate, nipping would-be school gangs in the bud.

The man at the helm of this espionage ring was the deputy head teacher, Mr Obura, whom the fraternity called FS (Flying Squad). The Flying Squad was an elite government unit established in 1992 to combat violent crime in Kenya. The then President, Mzee Daniel Toroitich Arap Moi, wanted to have his subjects under constant watch, having survived an attempted coup a decade earlier. Evidently, our school's version had borrowed something from the Head of State; using 'ears' in the form of *Jeshi la Mzee* (the old man's army) to mingle with citizens and gather data without their knowledge. It is from this concept that moles existed. Long before I put a face to the name, the jive painted him as a tyrant who saw every student as a potential threat to the institution's peace.

I was told he had studied mob psychology quite well to know that the mind of a teenager was fertile land, you just needed to sow seeds and the yield would be guaranteed. That was to say even the most innocent and naive were prone to being indoctrinated into weird religions, beliefs, drugs, sexual orientations, and gangs, a portend for disaster if you are taking care of over five hundred teenagers holed up in the same environment for months.

FS was patient, like a lion stalking a herd of antelopes in the thickets of the Maasai Mara. He was a reservoir of secrets, with evidence and a database so updated that he knew even minor issues such as shifting beds and with what intention. Statistics showed that no suspected delinquent stepped into his office and managed to walk out innocent.

"He is a bit short and slender, the size of an average Form Three, dresses like a student, and addresses everyone in a stern voice. He has a dark birthmark behind his left ear, and walks around with a bamboo stick."

That was the description I was given. *Wait a minute …*

Wasn't that the 'young man' who showed me to the canteen!
Holy Molly! I had run into the most feared man in Akili
and answered him rudely. I could visualize the witches,
who hate my progress back in Vihiga, conferring confetti
on each other to celebrate how much of dead meat I was.

I was informed that FS wore outfits that resembled our
uniform to blend in, like a leopard camouflaged atop a tree.
His investigations were top notch whenever there were
power blackouts, as student gatherings in the darkness
thrived on gossiping teachers, sharing disappointments
about the school, and planning mischief. Most of such
would be done over Cold Power shortened as CP; a
combination of cold water, drinking chocolate, sugar and
some cheap liquor called Sapphire. Making CP was akin
to assembling an aircraft, where the fuselage is made in
Brazil, engine comes from Rolls Royce in Germany and
the seats from China. The title had nothing to do with the
drink being made of cold water, rather it was a powerful
alcoholic brew served in a subterranean way to throw
snoops off balance. Additives like drinking chocolate and
sugar masked the smell and gave it a sweet taste, making
it easy to gobble without questionable facial expressions.
Sachets of unused Sapphire were concealed in shallow
graves sunk into flower beds, only dug out when needed
then buried back immediately.

To collect samples of the spiked beverage, FS would
join Cold Power sittings in the blackout, extend a cup of
his own and disappear before the lights came back. The
next day you would hear his famous line on assembly,
"it is either me or you who will go, and I am not going
anywhere." Those sentiments signalled that he had caught
wind of something fishy, and it was wise the recusants
dropped the idea as his patience had run out. The next time

he mentioned your name during assembly, while referring to the famous line, would be the day he is expelling you. Many would-be criminals reformed due to that threat, and even went ahead to pull very good grades in their final exams. That was the man on whose radar I had put myself the very first day, a harm's way that I was to either disentangle from or live under constant scrutiny.

Another name that came out conspicuously in my orientation was that of the school principal, who had been nicknamed Bokassa. Students of history will tell you that Jean-Bédel Bokassa was a controversial, and feared, military emperor of the Central African Republic, who acquired power through a coup. He was said to be a brutal leader, one who not only murdered his opponents, but also fed their remains to animals. The news was devastating as I had come here to break away from one dictator back home only to walk into the jaws two brutal ones. My fate was sealed.

DUBBING

EVERY EVENING, HORDES OF STUDENTS moved from dormitory to dormitory with plastic plates, begging colleagues for *Appe* (appetizer). Most sought was *Nyofnyof*, an interesting culinary creation and tradition that had been passed on from generation to generation within the student community. It was a homemade top-up where onions, tomatoes, garlic and spices were fried into a paste. This served as an additive to give the boring school food a mouth-watering taste. As time went by, it made sense why I was the centre of attention on my very first evening as everyone requested me to pick my share of the day's supper, and hand it over.

The unwritten rule was that a mono was not expected to eat Akili food on his first week of admission, since he had enough *Whales* (shopping) and was still full from eating well back at home. Thus, his body system was yet to adjust to communal diet. A *mono*, who lined up at the dining hall to eat school food during his first days was frowned upon. I mean, from which starved corner of the country did that one hail? What we did not know then was that some students came from really poor backgrounds, where eating was not guaranteed, so the school food was a blessing.

My research into that phenomenon revealed that older students loved it when *monos* forfeited supper, as there would be excess for them to be allowed to *dub*. Dubbing was the code name for the second share. In most cases, it was illegal as the catering department did an almost exact bill of quantities when preparing meals. So if five, ten, fifteen or more took more than their allocated plate, chances were that some students would miss. Missing a meal cut deeper than a heartbreak from first love. I almost cried the first time I missed food, and my heart has never healed that wound even decades later. Every time I remember that crushing evening, the wound festers, and my hearts bleed again as painfully as it did on that day.

Many a time I regretted for taking Mom for granted. At home, she would push or remind me that food was ready, and if I delayed for one reason or the other, my portion would be kept nicely covered on the kitchen table. I missed her patronage, her being on my back whenever I got reckless, but now she was not there. It was me against the world—if I did not go to meals in time, someone dubbed my share. High School panel-beat the crookedness out of me, the ruthlessness leaving rough edges in its wake.

Dubbing was such a serious transgression that the school had a chapter in its rule book dedicated to criminalizing it. It was theft, both from the school and parents, whose students would miss food they had paid for, so being caught dubbing was a non-negotiable two-week suspension. Upon returning, the culprit would replace whatever he had dubbed. If it was *ugali,* your only acceptable gate-pass back was a sack of maize. This rule was followed to the letter. I once witnessed a culprit report back with a cow after being caught dubbing beef. I have always wanted to know how his parents received him home with a suspension letter that required him to return to school with a live animal. We were on the assembly that morning when a cream pickup drove into the compound, and parked near the waiting bay. We were all oblivious of it until the cow mooed and we all turned our heads in the direction of the moo. The student was in the back of the pickup with the cow. That day it hit me that parenting is not easy.

The other punishment for dubbing preferred by prefects, but not in the official rules, was washing kitchen boilers or mopping the dining hall alone. It was painful and dehumanizing, but it saved one the drama of suspension as well as Bokassa admonishing you during assembly how uncouth you are to steal food, instead of better things like books.

"Imagine, a young man leaving his parents' home to come here and steal food, as if Akili is a fattening camp. These are the students who go home for holiday and the moment they step into the compound, their younger brothers and sisters run away because there will be no peace."

The dining hall prefects were tasked with mastering all faces that passed at the serving window, so that none appeared twice. However, there were students who were as good and they did it undetected almost every day. This would be made possible by changing appearances, like going in a shirt the first time, and coming back with a pullover, or vice versa. In every gang of four friends, one of them was a dub-pro, a much-needed connection to bridge the gap brought about by starvation.

Hunger led me to my first high school friend, Nahashon. He was diminutive, light skinned, with frail hands and a near-transparent skin through which you could see blood running in the veins. We had been admitted the same week, but he became well-known because everyone saw him as the school's last born. There was a joke that him being at Akili was tantamount to child labour, since he looked too young to be in high school.

Senior students nicknamed him 'Atom', a name fit for his size. He would be allowed to skip queues, exempted from manual work and pardoned whenever caught on the wrong, thus he got away with dubbing. We, his gang members, were to watch the prefects on duty, then update him on which queue to take and what direction to face. Our surveillance emboldened him to undertake his tasks, because he knew that if he was caught, the crew would help him do the punishment. We all celebrated when he emerged from the queue with food on the plate, having successfully staged another food heist. The loot would then be set before us to share.

Putting yourself in such a precarious position every day without raising alarm was the work of a genius. I know just how much Atom went through psychologically, as I tried my luck once and that remains my longest evening on the food queue in all my years at Akili. Even with the team cheering me on, I was a bag of nerves. Whenever I tried to act normal and chat up the next guy, a lump blocked my throat and my speech slurred. Someone on the same queue made things worse by talking about his colleague being busted the day before, and how he was clobbered by the cooks.

The geezer kept going on about the incident, even demonstrating how the culprit lifted his hands up in surrender. But I was hungry that day, hungrier than I had ever been, so the rumbling in my stomach gave me the courage to soldier on. If I was caught and suspended, that was fine, as the worst my parents would have done was kill me. The closer the queue moved forward the more droplets of pee soaked my pants. Every step forward had two outcomes: success or suspension.

My heart palpitated when I shifted my gaze only to see none other than FS standing at a corner of the dining hall. His eyes were busy scanning the food queue. He usually did walk-arounds in the dining hall, but for the first time the memory of our first ever meeting haunted me. My mind was certain I had let my guard down, and finally handed him that one precious chance to send me home. I had put so much effort into being in good books since I joined his hit list, but all that seemed to have come to an unceremonious end. How can you avoid capture from worse shenanigans only to be apprehended over food theft?

I finally made it to the service window, the long-awaited hour of victory or reckoning. My heart flapped against my ribcage like a caged bird as I extended my plate towards the cook. It was an aluminium plate, borrowed from a friend for better camouflage, since I had picked the first portion with mine, which was plastic. The cook dropped me a piece of *ugali* so hard that I lost grip of the plate and it fell to the floor *paaaaaa*! It rolled around in circles before tipping over while facing downwards. It dropped so loudly that everyone stopped what they were doing to observe. There I was, drawing attention at the worst possible time.

I could not begin to understand why it was so difficult to just remain calm, when the mission was almost over. It is said that the most dangerous moment in flying is at take-off and landing; but for dubbing, most culprits were nabbed midway, not at the service window.

I avoided looking at FS. Hardly had I knelt to ask for forgiveness when the cook apologized and asked that I hand him back the plate. That is the day I believed God really existed. Even with all the guilt, goofs and unwarranted attention, the one serving stew also poured a generous amount. I let out a sigh as I sat down at the table, not of relief but disbelief. I scanned the area one more time, and it was evident I bothered no one. I concluded that FS was on someone else's trail, and that is how I managed to slip through his fingers without alarm. It took me a bit of time to stop sweating, gather myself and get back to normal before digging into that food.

How Atom and company managed this every day remains a mystery, but I promised myself to never do that again. A student should not go through such mental torture for a meal. Maybe I was not meant to dub, or those who did it had become so institutionalized that they no longer feared the consequences. That partnership taught me that in life, even the most daring need a cheerleader, since it offers the much-needed confidence and courage to press on.

Nonetheless, no one was a villain in the eyes of fellow students for dubbing. We were all perennially hungry, just that the best of us lacked the mental strength to risk it, otherwise we would all dub. Again, the consequences were not worth one plate of food, especially for people like me whose parents would side with the teachers. They will not understand that you had no other option than to dub.

That explains why even after finishing the served food, the dining hall always had hundreds of students not leaving for class. They would be hovering around vantage points, licking their spoons with eyes glued to the diminishing queue. This is because once in a while, there would be excess and they allowed us to go for the surplus. The ready ones would jump on to the queue and serve all the remaining food.

Missing a portion of legal dub was heart-breaking, but nothing beat the pain of being served with bottom layer. The food had three layers—top, middle and bottom. Top layer was one we would long for as it had cooking oil, onions, and salt in perfect quantities thus delicious. Despite having a hideous green colour, you did not have to add spices for it to taste. Top layer was the reason some students forfeited games time to queue way before the bell rung. Being early also meant there were chances the cooks would request you to help them carry the food to the serving platform, and then reward you with extra portions. Top layer was a jackpot of a sort; it blanketed the plate with a thick layer of gravy, whose taste and aroma lasted to the next meal. Middle layer was just there; nothing much to say about it, but could be made better with a bit of *nyofnyof*.

The bottom layer was the depository of anything bad with the food—stones, weevils, and maggots all settled at the bottom. It was devoid of oil, the soup so dark that it resembled used gearbox oil, and full of crushed bones. It was hideous, tasteless, disgusting. However bad it was, you had no option than go for it if you didn't want to starve, unless you had enough pocket money to supplement with bread from the canteen. A would-be good day qualified as the worst if your place on the queue coincided with bottom layer. The weird bit about this so called bad food was that it may have tasted like garbage, but it was invaluable. I never at one point saw a student trip or fall and spill the food. You would topple, roll like a car tumbling down a cliff and still land with the plate facing up, food secure. You would have bruises on your elbows and traces of blood on the face, but the plate remained as intact as it had left the serving window. The starvation in boarding school turned us into magicians, and all this was attributed to one word: whistling.

WHISTLING TEAM

BESIDES THE DUB CHAMPION, THE second most important friend one needed to survive at Akili was a financier. In most cases, this would be a boy from a rich background, who could bankroll the group's mischief or lend you a few coins when you were flat broke. I found this in Francis whose father offered us a lift on reporting day. He was chubby-cheeked, short, dark, and plump from Nairobi. I was often tempted to touch his cheeks while shouting *abujubuju* like we do with babies. He was so heavy and round that his entire body shook whenever he laughed, and he was fond of laughing.

Francis had everything in plenty throughout the term: sugar, tomato sauce, drinking chocolate, money—name it. I never imagined that I would clear high school and leave him in form two. Francis's talents were not in books. He was always among the bottom ten performers every term, every year.

We nicknamed him Academic Angle, as he was always seen with threateningly huge textbooks. The books made him walk with a Tower of Pisa slant, but it seemed that his memory was a sieve. Or perhaps the teachers set the exam questions from the places he did not read. He reported to school every term on the first day, attended all lessons and sat for exams, but still scored his trademark zeros. Rumours had it that his parents had sacrificed him at the altar of voodoo for financial prosperity and, consequently, he would be dim like a torch with low batteries to continue being the family cash cow. His father instructed the school to only promote him to form three the year he dragged himself out of the bottom ten list, and the scion did not disappoint. When that happened, he secured one corner of the classroom, pitched his desk and sat there like a brooding chicken, his nose always buried in textbooks. Year after year, the school would have form one students come in, join him in form two, leave him there and exit while he remained, unbothered, unmoved.

He was not angry with anyone, he had the cleanest of hearts. So, when whistling checked in, he became the go-to person for me. Whistling was that unenviable period when all the pocket money was exhausted and you had to survive without bread. It was said that if you took porridge without chewing something your lips made you look like you were whistling.

As a matter of fact, over 80% of students who sneaked out of school were pushed into it by whistling. The problem resulted from childhood, where it was a taboo for children to have pocket money. Whatever our hands landed on that time was taken by our parents for 'safekeeping,' never to be seen again. If you tried asking for it, you would be reminded that the food you ate in their house was bought using money. So here we were; dumped in boarding school to exercise financial discipline with zero skills and experience on money management. At the same time, we grappled with other issues like protection fees asked by the senior students. We overspent from time to time and so we were penniless most of the time.

Watching your colleagues sink their teeth into bread while you whistled was painful. You felt abandoned by your parents, looked down upon by peers, mistreated by the system, and left to fate. It was embarrassing, given that students who whistled would all sit at one corner and offer emotional support to each other. They would watch from far as their counterparts with money devoured bread and other snacks. Some students would go to the canteen area and sip their tea in bits, while standing from afar to make peers think they were waiting for someone they had sent to get them bread, when in actual sense they were just trying to mask their ignominy. It was a tight rope to walk, and there was always the temptation of engaging in theft. However, too much pocket money that the rich kids had made them feel like they owned the world, so focus shifted from academics to pleasure.

Thus, we invented a new term: sensor. This was a tiny piece of bread pinched from a loaf to give you a 'sense' of how it tasted since you could not afford one. A sensor may have been tiny, but it boosted one's confidence in a way you cannot describe. Being denied a sensor by someone you considered a friend not only killed and hurt like a broken heart but also sometimes severed relationships. You knew who your real friend was by how they reacted to a sensor request. To remain afloat, students got recruited into yet another vice with a punitive clause in the school's rules book, *kudunga mshale* (hitting the target with an arrow). The idea behind *mshale* stemmed from a seemingly noble cause that everyone, including the administration, embraced from the onset.

A group of five students approached the school matron and tabled a proposal to help the catering department with minor assignments like setting up the tables, filling up cooking boilers with water, wiping the kitchen surfaces, and doing general cleanliness around the dining area. In exchange, they would be given the food that came back from the staffroom when teachers were done eating. It was a wonderful setup that saw hygiene standards in that department rise exponentially. Now, that was brilliant but the school had hundreds of students who would have done anything to enjoy such benefits. As word went around, the number grew from five, to seven, to ten, and then split into factions with members competing against each other.

As dissenting voices undermined the main group and innovated new ways to stay ahead, they expanded the concept to shine light on opportunities the kitchen staff could exploit for their own selfish needs. Soap was one of the most bought products in the school kitchen as cleaning boilers, surfaces, utensils, and uniform were essential. Each cook had his week of cleaning, a week he would be given money daily to procure soap. Initially, they all bought from the shops in Kiboswa. However, through *mshale*, students would give out soap bought by parents in exchange for food, and then the cooks would pocket the money given by the matron for the same.

Focus shifted from giving out food in exchange of cleaning services to soap. It was barter trade behind the kitchen every evening. It would begin with a student identifying who among the cooks seemed more approachable, then propose a secret rendezvous for the transactions. The exchange was like a drug deal—hand in the soap, pick food, clear off the scene. You also had to eat in hiding before being spotted by fellow students, as they would descend on that food like vultures.

You see, dubbing was a vice that only implicated the offending student. *Mshale,* on the other hand, put both student and cook in jeopardy, as once caught the student would suffer the usual suspension and food replacement and the cook lost their job. Nevertheless, instead of the consequences being deterrent, the *mshale* thrill made it a lucrative business. As a student gave out his own soap, his stock would be depleted. Then he would steal from friends and everyone else, and soon no one had soap. Therefore, *mshale* metamorphosed from barter to full blown business, where a plate of food was sold at twenty shillings.

The cash transactions pushed the business to the next level. This was even better for the cooks as evidence was in coins, which cannot be tied to the deal, unlike stolen soap which could be identified and confiscated, unless one was caught red-handed during the transaction. The surge in sales gave rise to a never-ending headache for the school matron, courtesy of the cooks hiding more food. Teachers started complaining that the portions taken to the staffroom were barely enough to feed them comfortably as before, and some even missed. Unless a student was from a family that gave him good pocket money, most of us would not afford more than ten of those before our cash ran out. So, a new approach was borne; that of four students coming together to cost share the bill then eat together. In the evenings, it was common to see students pottering around the kitchen trying to find like-minded individuals, who would pool resources together and grab the day's fill.

The risk with this amalgamation model showed when it was time to eat. There were fast and slow eaters. Some had the rare gift of being able to maw without chewing, regardless of how hot the food was. While you strove to be at par and eat the steaming hot food without burning your tongue, your partner had already swallowed four to five bites of the same. *Mshale* also watered down the measures that had been put in place to curb dubbing. A cook who always sold you food through the backdoor could not rut you out if he saw you taking a second portion. That was how dubbing levels hit an all-time high as a third of the population missed food every evening, and the more the matron increased food rations, the lesser people fed. To mitigate this, the school introduced meal cards. It was a brilliant move, as it helped the school force students with huge fee arrears to prevail upon their parents to pay up or miss food.

Notwithstanding, Akili always suffered progressive degradation in almost everything that seemed futuristic. Having a meal card that was not yet ticked on a particular day meant you had not eaten; therefore, eligible to walk into the kitchen and demand your portion. So even as this document instilled order in the dining hall, it also opened loopholes that only geniuses could exploit, and Akili was not in short supply of those. These individuals found a way of covering the card with very light cello tape so that the tick would not stick. This gave them a chance for another round. Others would go to the school bursar and claim to have lost their cards. They were issued with a new one, which was then used to pick two meals without being accused of dubbing. In that instant, meal cards became the most priced commodity in the school, more than the usually valuable mugs and plates.

In a man-eat-nothing society like Akili High School, you would be forgiven for stealing a colleague's book, pen or seat, but not their mug or plate. You could not have a good night's sleep knowing that you lacked a mug for the next day's porridge. This is because you would have to sit aside and watch as others got served while you waited for a willing friend to finish and lend you his.

The mugs and plates were cool though; they had graphics and words emblazoned on their surfaces—swastikas, charts, nicknames, even girlfriend's names for those who were much ahead in that department. Such branding was a sure way of tracing your items whenever they got lost. Baron's mug was, for instance, inscribed with the name SHILLA, his girlfriend.

Where the kitchen failed, the canteen made up in earnest, coming through for students whose hunger pangs were past normal food and *mshale*. Our canteen was a tiny round colonial structure that sat right behind the school kitchen. It was built by the missionaries, who started the school in 1954, forty-five years before I joined. The walls, roof and paint had deteriorated over time, leaving a dilapidated structure in which rain water oftentimes leaked through.

The school did not have many students when the missionaries built it, but over the years it had grown into a well performing educational centre, attracting young men eager to learn far and wide. The canteen, thus, had become too small to comfortably cater for the large number of students, but the administration did not see it wise to expand it. Only two items were sold there—loaves of bread cut into four quarters nicknamed *todhi*, and buns (*chura*). Both products cost a standard five shillings. The name *chura* was borne out of the rough skin the buns had; they were round and the size of an adult toad.

Whereas the bread was delivered hot from a bakery nearby, *churas* were cooked on site by a neighbour who doubled up as a parent to my classmate, Alex. The business educated Aleckii, his siblings as well as resourced the household. Being the son to Mama Chura, as she was called, gave the boy many friends, genuine and fake, all trying to be close enough to hopefully get a free bun on days they were broke. Being friends with Aleckii was akin to marrying into royalty going by how precious *churas* became around week eight of the school term when everyone was penniless.

The tiny window through which people ordered from was a victim of assault every morning as students scrambled for bread. The scrum was occasioned by everyone jostling to buy in a limited time because, once the bell rang, you had to be in class in time. Small and less muscular students like me watched from a distance as everyone jostled through the tight mass to get to the window, get their piece and scramble out again. The well-built ones threw their bodies into the melee and bought whatever they wanted, while the clever ones would lift each other like gymnasts, so that the one at the top approached the window from above the crowd. It was difficult to force your way out of so many bodies once you got your bread. By the time you broke free, the bread would be in pieces. Somehow, these broken pieces were never seen even after the crowd dispersed; it was as if imaginary people gobbled them before they reached the ground. Additionally, you had to hold your coins tightly in your palm lest they too got lost in the commotion.

Regardless, this presented an opportunity for

entrepreneurial minds to make a killing. They woke up earlier than everyone else, bought several buns then sold them to fellow students at an extra shilling. In essence, such individuals got a free bun for every five buns they sold. A strong team comprising rugby players offered to get into the scramble as long as one bought them bread. The problem with this trick was that the guy would sometimes take too many orders, then forget the faces of those who sent him, which was a recipe for disagreements during distribution.

There were also unscrupulous fellows who took your money, got into the melee, bought the stuff and disappeared into thin air, leaving you waiting for nothing. It would dawn on you that you have been conned when the bell rang and the crowd cleared, but the person you sent was nowhere.

On the other hand, the chaos also proved a daunting task for the shopkeeper; he had to ensure he gave the correct order to the correct hand among the many extended his way. Almost every day, a conniving student would join the melee, stretch out an empty hand and claim the money had dropped somewhere inside the canteen. He would hang on that lie until he was given a *chura*. The administration always tried to impose a rule on people queuing for the service, but it never worked. It was as if scrambling made the experience complete.

The biggest mistake a shopkeeper would make was to get engrossed in the crowd at the front window, and forget to close the door, as a stampede would barge in abruptly and cart away the stock. It had happened several times before, and even though there were suspects, no one had tangible evidence against the perpetrators. I have always reasoned that that scramble for services symbolised the world that awaited us once we were done with high school, where we would have knowledge, but still have to fight for opportunities. The devious buyers represented the difficult employers and clients we would encounter along the streets, while the run-down structure stood for Kenya's ailing economic system.

EDGE OF GLORY

THE CODE OF SILENCE AMONG students in Akili was as tight as a pack of thieves. Getting an eye witness or informer to back up a claim against a fellow student was almost impossible. Only FS knew how to make people talk or confess, otherwise any other teacher would spend hours grilling would-be witnesses and informers but get nothing tangible. It was inculcated in us as early as the first year that as long as you were a student, you would be found in some transgression. Therefore, telling on your colleague would haunt you someday.

The reason FS always turned his informers into prefects was to have them protected by the school, and also have a moral obligation to tell the truth. The mastermind also ensured that before people knew who the informers were, they had received immunity. Becoming a prefect moved you one step closer to the administration; however, it set you against the civilians you had been close to. Prefects were a mixture of brilliance, talent, size and religious orientation, with different departments being allocated one based on their requirements.

Dining hall crew was synonymous with heavily built boys, who had the stature to scare colleagues from dubbing. Guidance and counselling was always left to a student from Christian Union (CU); a student who showed genuine leaning and love for God. One who had the ability to sit a peer down and give him a heart to heart without prejudice; not a random thug who would counsel you today and sneak out the following day to eat *matumbo* (tripe) in Kiboswa. Most of us were of questionable character, which rendered this the most difficult position for the administration to fill.

The irony is that Akili High is a mission school, sponsored by the Pentecostal Assemblies of God Church, which is also home to one of the biggest Bible training colleges in western Kenya. Different institutions shared a fence with the school: The Sanctuary is to the North; Akili Primary to the East; and Akili Bible College (ABC) to the West. I was on punishment to weed flower beds around the science laboratories when I stumbled upon a glaring loophole in the security system. Whereas the fence on every other side of the school compound was prohibitively high and bolstered with thick *kayapa* (Kei-Apple), the one bordering the church was low and thin, making it porous.

It was obvious that students who sneaked out through this channel jumped over the fence, landed into the chapel's compound, then proceeded to the main road via the wide-open gate. The discovery was unexpected, but I made a mental note of it if I ever needed a prison break.

At that point, there was no reason to sneak out as I was beginning to accept and fit into the Akili way of life. As a matter of fact, I had so much faith in the education system and my parents. I considered breaking out of school would be a stab in their back, so I was comfortable behind those giant gates.

My cradle was, however, rocked when I fell in love with a pair of crisp white Air Force One sneakers belonging to Yobra, an anagram of Brayo (Brian). Yobra did not mind selling them to me; however, forking out three thousand Kenya shillings from the meagre pocket money my parents gave me was like milking stones. Unless I diverted part of my school fees towards that purchase, I would never raise such an amount.

For reasons best known to them, my parents had been paying fees into the school account, and only gave me the bank slip to present to the school bursar. Otherwise, if I got the fee at that time, it would have gone to those shoes. At least, I would have been killed after wearing the shoes of my dreams. I entered into a deal with Brayo that he would lease the shoes to me at five hundred shillings over the holidays to go 'threaten' a few villagers with.

I did not have the five hundred on me, so the terms were that I pay half on closing and the balance upon return on opening day. Brayo had several sneakers, so he did not mind making some extra money on a pair I would return in a few weeks. The deal was signed, shoes handed over in excellent form and my remaining pocket money, including fare, crossed over into his wallet. I would have trekked home that closing day if Bokassa had not offered the school bus to help transport those going my direction. We squeezed into the bus like people on an asylum trip, putting up with each other's acrid stench until we got to our destinations.

I stomped Mbale town in the whitest pair of shoes anyone had ever seen, feeling like I had won the lottery. On other closing days, I alighted and headed straight home, but this one was different. I strutted across the town walking all the time to ensure that I would be seen by many people. The shoes announced my presence—I could hear sighs from people whenever I passed, adding a spring to my walk.

The last time I had been in shoes that attracted such rapt attention was a decade earlier as a primary school boy when Mom bought me the only pair in the whole school. The difference was that whereas the earlier pair elicited hate and the name 'The Boy with Shoes,' this one brought positive vibes. It was a statement that Madam Jane's son was in a provincial school not only mingling with exposed fellows, but also enjoying the finer things in life.

People who saw me that day must have concluded that I was wealthy, because a society will judge people by what they display, even when they do not own it. We revere individuals who drive top of the range SUVs, which are probably hired or bought with stolen public money. They would then look down upon others, who own simple sedans they have worked so hard and genuinely to acquire. The same phenomenon is replicated during elections as we ignore would-be genuine leaders because they look poor. In retrospect, we vote for those who sell themselves as affluent, overlooking the fact that they could be flashing cash from bank loans. The loans are later repaid probably with public money once these cunning aspirants clinch their positions of interest. Genuine wealth should be subtle.

I really put on airs that day, but my fifteen minutes of

fame did not last that long. Someone spotted me scurrying around town boisterously and informed Mom to expect a pompous son in the evening. She met me outside the house and the shoes were her first point of reprimand before I even put my bag down:

"You have now officially become an adult who can afford expensive shoes, right? I can't have peace as everyone is coming to report how my son is a nuisance in Mbale. On that note you'll pay your own fees next term."

I stood there and listened to the ranting, patiently waiting for her to finish. I yearned to go inside the house and make myself comfortable. I thought of informing her that I had just leased the shoes for a short period to look good, but her demeanour stopped me. History had shown me that once her mind was made up, throwing in a contrary opinion made things worse.

The shoes needed to be wiped since I had stepped on all manner of dirt during my show at the market, and one of the clauses in the lease agreement was to keep them sparkling clean. I removed them, wiped the leather surface with a damp cloth, and then propped the pair to lean on a surface and dry. I went into the kitchen and landed on what was the best welcome meal anyone could have given me— boiled maize. I pulled out three cobs from the stovetop, placed them on my plate and found a quiet corner where I could gorge without Mom's eyes constantly hovering over me.

I was headed to throw away the cobs when my eyes fell on Bobby, our brown Kenyan Shepherd, carrying one of those shoes in his mouth. I shouted his name, to which he turned, dropped the shoe and ran over like a child rushing for a hug from a returning mother. His tail was wagging, body shaking and the eyes beaming with excitement.

Bobby was not just an ordinary mongrel in the village, he was my boy. I lost count of the number of times he accompanied me on night vigils at funerals. Bobby would sit in the nearby bushes until I was ready to go back home for him to keep guard.

Someone had once poured dirty water on us as we waited for a friend to join us, and Bobby stayed on without blinking an eye. The only instance he let me down was one night when another bigger dog chased us and Bobby ran away so fast that he left me behind. I found him waiting for me near our house, but I had since forgiven him.

I walked over to where he had dropped the shoe, his tail still wagging vigorously, hitting my legs. Bobby had sunk his teeth deep into the shoe while carrying it. There were visible grooves, which could not be washed away. On closer inspection, I discovered more ruin. The tongue-like flap at the front was chewed, and the Nike tick had been sheared into pieces. The laces ravaged into a mound of what resembled cooked spaghetti. A shoe that had been so beautiful and clean now looked like a wreck pulled from a fatal collision.

My eyes welled. I contemplated on whether to scorn him for ruining the shoe, or revel in the excitement of seeing him happy to have me back. The innocence in his eyes made it difficult for me, but the damage was done. Hitting him would have done very little, if anything, to help the situation. What I needed was a strategy to make three thousand shillings before opening day to pay Yobra and retain the pair. However, my actions had landed me into deep trouble, since there was a declaration that I would pay my fees the following term.

REMISS

On All Opening Days, Mom always left for work assured that around midday I would shower, dress up and head straight to school. Things were different on this day, though. The tide changed direction when she made clear her declaration that I would have to pay for my own upkeep. She gave me two hundred shillings for pocket money, shopping, and fare back to school. My spirited attempts to squeeze out more were in vain. We ended up brawling. In her books, I was not concentrating on education. "Will you be able to afford this luxurious life you love after you finish school?"

As I sat in that van headed back to school, I pictured a long penniless term ahead, a life of whistling I had outgrown. To distract myself, I passed our school and went to Kisumu where George, the fourth member of our gang, lived. He was not one of the sharpest in class, but he scrapped by with a bit of cramming here and a *mwakenya* there, an art he had perfected. *Mwakenya* was a term used in Kenya's political scene. It referred to top secret material that proponents of multi-party democracy exchanged amongst themselves to operate under the government's radar. It had to be on very tiny pieces of paper for stealth.

That is how the name found its way into the academic world as students, who did not trust their memories, sneaked little folded papers with shorthand answers into exam rooms as a backup. It was a different ballgame for girl schools: instead of papers, they scribbled answers on their thighs and palms, making it difficult to be detected. How they managed to lean over and peep at their thighs in search of answers during the exam is a mystery.

George was the uncontested king of *mwakenya* at Akili, and the street rat our gang needed to survive. He always had his ears on the ground, and knew the happenings in the school's underbelly to ensure we stayed four steps ahead of the law. Most students who were caught in mischief lacked this connection. I knew George during our first week in form one, when his box was burglarized butterfly-style, and all his valuables were stolen, including his underwear, leaving him with only the pair he was wearing. He was light complexioned, had wide teeth protruding out of his gums, ears so big and extended that he reminded me of baby cups with handles on both sides, and he spoke in monotone.

Getting permission out of the school as a Mono was difficult because the administration interpreted it to be homesickness. So, he had to survive with wearing one underwear the whole term. He wore it during the day and washed it at night, and then put it on the next morning. He approached me to help him with one pair if I had a new one because his had not dried the previous night, otherwise he would wear it moist. I gave him one of mine, though he never told me whether it fit him. That remains the first and only time I have shared, of all things, underwear, but it was the beginning of a bosom friendship that lasted my entire stay at Akili. The brutal introduction to the system changed him; he became temperamental like a gorilla, uncontrollable when he got annoyed. He was henceforth baptized 'Lethal.'

Lethal was always baying for blood, ready to face the enemy head on, even when some situations appeared way beyond our abilities. He was on record for hitting some villager's head with a stone, almost cracking his cranium, due to a fight over water at the river. The gang nicknamed me Oblong because of the shape of my head—it is ovate on the left forehead. The gospel according to Lethal was that being a first born, my mom was still a novice; therefore, she was unaware my head needed a reshape the day I was born. This is because babies come out with uneven skulls pressed by the womb.

I had never noticed that deformity until Lethal pointed it out. From then on, it became a constant point of concern for me, especially when I spoke to someone and they seemed to stare at my head. It is a name I hated as it reminded me of a blemish I had no remedy, but then a nickname was the only way to remain part of the coterie. It is stupid to engage in mischief, and keep referring to each other using official names.

Lethal preferred staying with his uncle in Kisumu's densely populated Kondele estate over the holidays, rather than go to his parents' home in Keroka. His host was young and liberal. Furthermore, the said uncle did not have many responsibilities yet, so he gave him more pocket money.

There was a more affectionate reason, which topped the two above though: Milkah. Lethal was exploring the world of sex with his uncle's housemaid. While he was barely sixteen, Milkah was in her mid-twenties, a mother of one. She was married at some point, but sought divorce. Lethal mentioned that it all began as a joke when the uncle went on a night out leaving the two at home alone. They watched a movie that had erotic scenes, and before they could wrap their minds around what was happening, it was bollocks into the hoo-ha.

As much as both knew they had crossed into a dangerous territory, it was difficult to hold back, so they decided to let themselves loose. Lethal, just like the rest of us, was a novice in sex at the time, so the much he did was get hard, undress, then wonder what to do next. The maid, boasting several years of practice, took it upon herself to guide him on where to place his little winy, and make movements with his body. The boy was confused, excited, and curious all at once, but that act set in motion a relationship that would take a break when schools opened and continue over the holidays.

To bolster his skill set, she also introduced him to pornographic films, which they would watch, pick new skills and try out. Milkah later reconciled with her estranged husband and resigned from her work, leaving Lethal suicidal, but with a wealth of *sexperience* most of us could only dream of.

The house to Lethal's uncle was a two-bedroom bachelor pad with brown leather seats, a 21-inch television, water dispenser, and a VCD player sitting on top of the TV. In the early 2000s, those were possessions that only existed in households whose owners were doing well financially. Coincidentally, Atom too had decided to alight in Kisumu, and pass by Lethal's place before going to school. The only missing member was Academic Angle, but that was expected. It was his father's tradition to drop him to school back-left in one of the family cars. It was the first time I was introduced to blue movies.

Lethal and his darling housemaid had over time compiled a number of episodes. The three of us sat in that house and watched as different sets of couples came on set, undressed, made out and got down to business with all action captured from different camera angles. The female actors were gorgeous vixens with sexy eyes, flawless skins, mermaid-shaped bodies, and thick compact boobies. For some reason, the male counterparts had a rugged look; bald, muscled, and heavily pierced, with silver studs popping out of their ears. Their toned bodies, covered in all manner of tattoos, shone like fish out of water. They looked like bulls preparing to mate.

There was very little tenderness in the way they handled those beauties, who, contrary to my expectation, seemed to enjoy being roughed up, slapped, and even choked. The look in their eyes portrayed confusing thoughts for me— although inexperienced, I expected the act to be mushy, romantic, and slow; not the acts of mild violence I was watching. The room was dead quiet, concentration levels higher than what I saw from these two in class, especially the *mwakenya* connoisseur. If only watching porn had exams.

I was so hard that my mind started getting ready for the moment my thing would burst at the seams or disengage and fall off. Lethal informed me that the only way to calm myself down was to take a cold shower, a trick that worked, but my mind refused to let go of the images. Thanks to Milkah, the boy had become a specialist. I wondered whether he intended to follow that as a career path. When I think about that day, I realize how awkward it was, but once again another new chapter had been born in my life. The thrusts, sighs, and moans became embedded in my mind; exposure that put sexual fantasies in my head and made me desire more.

From that day on, I was always looking out for adult videos to watch and quench an insatiable thirst that had not existed before. In the months that followed, I careened so deep into pornography that I started researching on how things work, both in real life and on set. As I dug deeper, it occurred to me that the latter was all stage acting; entertainment that had little benefit. The sets, sound effects and props put into creating those films spiced them for the viewers, but not many real-life sex escapades applied that knowledge. Furthermore, a substantial number of their scripts seemed to border on violence against women— bondage, use of force, slaps, and insults, something that did not augur well with me because I had younger sisters.

Imagining that someone's daughter made money sucking gonads on camera for a few dollars made me sick. My once curious mind started gravitating away from *sextainment*, so I left it to those, who were okay with the content. It was a spirited battle within, since I had become addicted, but I managed to forego the short-term reward for conscience's sake.

As the day wore on, Lethal proposed that we catch a beer before reporting for school. He took the car keys from his uncle's bedroom and huddled us into the white Subaru Leone. I had seen it parked outside the house. I did not even know he could access its keys, leave alone gain the courage to drive it in a populated suburb. He was having trouble multitasking between the clutch and keeping an eye on the road. Severally, the car jerked furiously, took off at high speed, or stalled, then he would crank it again and continue his guesswork.

We missed running into several pedestrians by a whisker, and they would hurl insults in Luo as we grazed past in laughter. But we didn't understand the language. The allure of being in a 'stolen' car driven by an unlicensed learner was so fascinating that it gave us goose bumps. One day was turning out to be more memorable than my entire holiday, never mind that we were playing Russian roulette with our lives.

After almost hitting an electricity pole, ramming into someone's bumper and driving off the scene, we managed to ease into an empty parking spot at a tavern. Lethal killed the engine, accomplishment written on his face. I could not openly admit that beer was still a new territory to me as my friends were home and dry with it. Atom, the son to Bishop Nyavanga and smallest boy at Akili, took Guinness. Lethal ordered a Tusker, while my heart stuck with Pilsner since it had the avatar of a lion; a symbol of my name.

To me, the beer had an unpleasant taste; I wondered what fun these two derived from it. I almost vomited every time I took a gulp, but I wanted to make my gang proud, so I soldiered. Atom and Lethal must have noticed I was struggling because they kept urging me on;

"Take liquor, Oblong, this is the stuff real men are made of."

By the time I had emptied the bottle, my head was spinning, images were hazy, and I could not comprehend anything. If whatever I craved to say actually came out, I would have brought that club to a standstill with the enormous English words flooding my mind. Up until that point, I had never known my vocabulary was rich with words so complicated that they scared me. No one got to hear them as my speech was slurred, and every time I tried to stammer through, I would hiccup so viciously that they disappeared. What kept me at peace was that even though I was wasted, blurry images of my gang kept crossing my eyes, so I knew my safety was guaranteed.

BUTTERFLY EFFECT

I HAVE NO RECOLLECTION OF how and in what state the Subaru got back to Kondele, or the time we checked into school that day. I only remember waking up late in the night to find myself in my dormitory bed. The inebriation had frittered slightly from my system, but I had vomited, smelled badly, and my head was pounding. I was ravenous since my last meal was back at home before leaving, after which I spent the afternoon feeding my lust and ego. That was me at rock bottom; such a nasty feeling I thought I would die that night. Somehow, Atom and Lethal had brought a drunken student through the gate, signed him in and tucked him in bed without raising alarm.

As I cleaned my mess, I took some minutes to think about the events leading to this moment. My mind remembered the unresolved shoe issue, so my nocturnal brilliance proposed one last ditch effort. That was to write a letter to Thatcher explaining that she had overreacted, and imposed on me an unwarranted punishment based on conjecture. I would inform her that the controversial shoes were not only leased, but also Bobby had reined terror on one. That meant I had to replace the whole pair.

After breakfast, I sat at my desk. In fine English, I drafted a letter expressing how I had been working so hard in school lately as per my grades, but the spirit was not replicated in pocket money. I was tired of being the poor soul among my peers, so Mom either had to step up or see my grades plummet. I sealed the enveloped, addressed it, corrupted a used stamp with toothpaste, and then dropped it for post before settling into school for the term. Thank God, Yobra was one of those students who never reported back on the first week of opening; it gave me a bit of breathing space. The pressure was still on as I was low on pocket money, part of which I had even bought beer with.

In my belief, Thatcher would see the persistence and add me more pocket money, which I would use to pay for the shoes, sell part of my shopping to raise the balance, and then find ways to survive until she visited.

A reply came towards the end of that week:

Dear Beloved Son,

You are not studying for me as I already have a good job myself. I grew up in a poorer family and went to school without pocket money, but still excelled. If you fail exams, do not show your face in this compound.

Mom

That was it. She had thrown me under the bus again. Was she aware I was still within the confines of school since I chose not to exploit the weak link in security? Was she aware that going forward I would be forced to start waking up earlier than usual and sleeping late as Yobra would be lingering around my bed asking for his shoes? Did anyone care to know that I had tried and exhausted all the legal channels to solve this money issue, yet my efforts kept being dimmed unceremoniously? After all was said and done, would I be wrong for resolving to look at the other side of the coin? Desperate times call for desperate measures. The battle lines had been drawn, long and thick. Yours truly was *jomping* (sneaking out of the school) that week to look for money; if I die, I die.

I discovered that when sneaking out, you should always inform a trusted friend so that he covered for you; of course you had to pay him immediately you snuck back in. Statistically, those who had sneaked got caught and were expelled did it alone. A case in point was Amos, whose home was a ten-minute walk from Akili. He was in the habit of sneaking out to go and have warm showers at home, eat, and visit his girlfriend who was in a day school nearby. The catastrophic mistake he made repeatedly was not informing anyone whenever he exited, so class and dormitory prefects kept filling him as absent with no one to alibi him. As fate would have it, one of his escapades coincided with a planned strike that was botched midway.

Memories of that Saturday night are still fresh on my mind like morning dew. We were jolted from slumber by stones landing on the roofs of our dormitories. Waking up to such noise remains one of the most horrifying moments in my entire stay at Akili. It was pitch black, the blackout a coincidence. Being in the Western part of Kenya, we were not short of superstitious individuals who quickly concluded that some evil person had finally managed to put our school on visitation by djinns, locally referred to as *majini*.

The fact that Akili School was near Lake Victoria made it even more believable for people like me who grew up in Vihiga, where villagers beat drums every December to cast out *majini* and send them to where they belonged—the lake. The word *majini* is Swahili for 'under water', thus it was believed that the djinns lived under water. *Who told me to enrol into a school close to the lake?*

We huddled together, trembling, as the sound of falling rocks rent the air. Staying in a dormitory as old as Kilimanjaro was even more terrifying; if the pelting continued, the roof would cave in. My heart flapped in my ribcage. I even swore to join the Christian Union if we got out alive, maybe it was time to put the old me behind and become a trusted soldier of Christ. After an hour or so, the horror stopped. It went eerily silent you could hear your neighbour breathing. None of us moved, just in case the evil spirits decided to continue.

When we were convinced all was over, we hobbled outside to the sight of a police cruiser and several cops. The siren was off, but the strobe lights were flashing to reveal six silhouettes of police officers. We did not know what had happened, just murmurs that the police had thwarted a strike. Information was scanty but everyone was a suspect.

The first suspects were apprehended that night, but the rest slipped away. They spent the night at the police station assisting the police with investigations. In Africa, that description means having your balls squeezed until your sperm count drops to zero. By the time you leave the station, if you walk out alive that is, your manhood will never rise to the occasion. Through confessions from those arrested, the cops were able to weave together a timeline of events leading to the near-tragic night.

The plan had been to set the furniture store, library and administration block on fire, and then pelt the dormitories to wake up the school's lemmings. The entire school would then come aboard. What we had initially thought to be a blackout was not. The buggers had cut off power from the main switch to enable them operate under the cover of darkness. To be fair to the group, this was the biggest intelligence fail by FS. Had it not been for a breakdown in communication, the school was a few minutes short of going ablaze.

The boys revealed that one of them sent a signal prematurely, prompting the team with stones to hit our roofs before the targeted buildings were flared, otherwise they had all been dowsed in petrol. With everyone awake, including teachers, a call was made to the nearby police post, and cops arrived in time to botch the strike. The structures were spared by a whisker, but that was close. The first order FS issued was that every dormitory captain takes roll call and forward the list the same night.

In the morning, an accountability exercise was undertaken by comparing names of students in the dormitory that night against those who had valid leave out. Any trouble maker on the radar of FS, me included, was called to the staffroom and grilled for hours. You were to say anything suspicious you have ever heard, spotted or been involved in, as well as colleagues you thought were disgruntled enough to consider a strike. If your name popped out of several lips, you moved into the red zone, a bad thing for loud mouths. Many of them found themselves entangled in the mess.

Amos happened to have sneaked out earlier that day, so his name was neither on the list from the dormitory, infirmary, nor leave out. Since no one came forward to explain that he was just a petty offender, who could never partake in a felony the magnitude of a strike, he was among those expelled that Sunday. I was not about to make such a mistake, so I confided in Lethal regarding my plans to *jomp*. I requested him to watch my back as well as gather any information I may need on my return. Since it was a favour he was returning, I trusted him. With my tracks well covered and resolve high, it was time to bring the idea to fruition.

That evening, I went back to survey the fence and confirm my eyes had not played tricks on me the last time I was there. Certainly, the barbed wire was still low and porous enough to climb across. Will check; fare check; way check, or whatever it was. I was now in real Akili business.

JOMPING

AFTER SUPPER, I WENT AROUND either saying hello or doing things to be noticed by prefects. I also appeared before the suspected spies for them to confirm that I was present. I even 'tripped' and fell right in front of the head boy, prompting him to come over and help lift me up. I was not worried about the administration. Mr Khangati, a trainee carefree teacher full of antics was on duty that week. We had nicknamed him *Chizi* (mad man).

Having done all the groundwork, I informed my class prefect that I was headed to the library for the evening preps. The planned time of departure was between 7.45 p.m. and 8.00 p.m. It was not too early to raise suspicion, and not too late to sneak out and miss vehicles. I sat in the library for a few minutes and had a chitchat with the librarian as my eyes observed the wall clock. At half past seven, I excused myself and sauntered towards the fence.

Lights in all the laboratories were on, but there was no sign of life save for one moth that seemed to have a field day, levitating from one building to the other drawn by the misty fluorescent tube bulbs. There was one last thing left—to dump the uniform. Anyone who would meet me dressed in Akili outfits outside the school compound at night would put two and two together and know that I was up to some mischief.

For a moment, I pondered over everything, sort of a risk analysis, with a voice telling me to drop the whole idea and head back to class. But then I reflected on how I'd come too far to bail out, and the more time I was wasting on indecision, the bigger the chances of getting caught. I broke a branch off one of the nearby trees, and used it to dig a little vault in the flowerbed. I removed my shirt, pressed it into a small heap, and put it into the earth before gathering soil over it like a cat covering its poop.

I was left with school shoes, trouser, and a black vest that I had worn under the shirt to help me camouflage. The pullover was tied around my waist. It flowed down to my buttocks. I had tied it like a professional mourner in my village. Nevertheless, I was still within the school laws, unless a clause against being shirtless existed. My eyes did one final scan to ascertain the coast was clear before crossing into freedom. There was grave silence everywhere.

I stretched out my right hand, grabbed the wooden pole and lifted myself off the ground. Soon my feet were searching for barbed wire support with the help of light rays wafting from the laboratories. A wire at a time, I managed to get to the top of the pole. I took some time to calculate my descend lest my feet got entangled in the lines. If I fell from that position, chances were that I would crimp my neck, break my legs, or both.

I flung my body across the fence. I landed on the other side and planted my feet firm on the ground. I looked up to find I had touched right next to the main door of the Pentecostal church. Through that door, walked a priest every Sunday, preaching to the congregation about living in the ways of the Lord. Through that door, went altar boys carrying wafers that were converted to sacrament that would be taken by sinners who were turning over a new leaf. Out of that door, strolled individuals filled with God's grace and hope for eternal life after a moving sermon. Through that door, should have been Hillary loping towards the altar, to repent and have my name written in the Book of Life.

On the other side of that door, there was a new life I should have been leading, but here I was scuttling past like an animal headed to an abattoir. I did not care about church doors and salvation at that point. Push had come to shove, and I needed to be out of school for the sake of my sanity, and by extension, life.

A cold night wind kissed my face as I strolled majestically out of the church compound to the bus stage. My mind was a hodgepodge of thoughts, wondering whether the re-entry would be as seamless as the exit had been. I was like a space shuttle, launched into interstellar space on a mission, but whose safe return was not guaranteed.

It was one thing to successfully *jomp*, another to slither back unnoticed, and a more critical one to disappear and blend back in without some nosy bastard noticing your absence. I regretted my decision because, at that point, I was officially an offender and a candidate for suspension without negotiation. Apart from that, my parents would have to buy two rolls of barbed wire for the school. A roll was about 3,000 shillings (roughly 30 dollars), a figure six times as much pocket money as I was given every month, so two rolls made it 6,000. That is separate from the 3,000 shillings for the shoes I was sneaking out to search for. It translated to a sum of NINE THOUSAND SHILLINGS in total. This meant that pocket money would be withheld for so many months that I would probably die in school ... that is if my parents did not kill me themselves.

But did I care? There comes a time when the risk trounces the fear of death, the adrenalin shooting you to the space like a rocket. For years, I had tried to be a good student, only engaging in small-time mischief like nicking shirts, watching porn, and drinking. Now I had crossed the line into the next level of misdemeanour. If I bumped into a teacher at this hour, since most lived around, my goose was cooked.

Just the week before, Ken Mike, who hailed from the neighbourhood, had sneaked out to attend the funeral vigil of someone he knew around the school. He arrived there without any incident, only to get carried away and join a group of drummers trying to keep the night warm. Coincidentally, that happened to be the night cops on patrol had been on the trail of some village thieves who were believed to have run off and taken refuge among the mourners. Ken came back to school sweating, without shoes, and covered in red soil from top to bottom.

Kiboswa was dead that night, nothing close to the bustling market with women chirping loudly during the day. Only two shops had yellow lights flickering below their fascia boards; the rest were pitch black, the kind of darkness loved by muggers. This was not the hour to waste time choosing the best vehicle, so I hopped into the first one that stopped. Hardly had I made myself comfortable in the seat behind the driver when my eyes spotted a familiar burly figure with a conspicuous goatee. It was Mr Omosh, a mathematics teacher at Akili, who, thankfully, taught a different stream from mine, so we did not interact a lot at close range while in school. I hoped that his heavy lens glasses were for bad eyesight which would be worse at night. I had heard rumours that he owned a *matatu* on the Kisumu – Kakamega route that I had never bothered to know its registration number. If I knew the registration number beforehand, I would have let it pass and waited for the next one, but I was already aboard and requesting to alight would have attracted attention to me, something I did not want.

Mr Omosh was at the front passenger seat. He was chatting with the driver while seemingly reconciling the day's books of accounts. For the first time, I appreciated the fact that public service vehicles overloaded; we kept stopping intermittently to pick more passengers. This was good and bad in equal measure. Good that the more crowded we were the harder it was to be noticed, but bad as Mr Omosh kept craning his neck to survey the cabin whenever a new passenger got on.

Every time he threw his face in our direction, I felt his eyes boring into mine. The safest thing for me was to look outside the window, so that my face was obscured and our eyes did not meet. Throughout the journey, I stared into the dark world zooming past with its good and evil.

I heaved a sigh of relief when I alighted at my destination. Mr Omosh had not noticed that a vessel he owned had successfully aided a student in sneaking out of the school he taught. My first stop was at Voke's. His official name was Kevin, but the boys in the 'hood shortened it to Kevo. Somehow, they felt that was not enough and mutilated it further by inverting it so that we pronounced it from backwards as Voke. I knocked on his door in the code we used—three light taps, a scratch, then a knock.

From childhood, Voke was into electronics when the rest of us were breaking limbs and nursing bruises from the football pitch. His formal education ended at primary school; thereafter, he honed his electrical and electronic skills through apprenticeship from an engineer in Mbale. He quickly built a name as a go-to person for electrical installations and repairs, but then he discovered *chang'aa* and embraced it with both arms. His star had started taking a downward spiral as more of his clients sought sober service providers.

I was praying he was not out drinking since my visit was impromptu. Luckily, he was not only home having supper, but was also sober. That meant one thing—he was broke, his drinking circle too, and they had accumulated more debt for the brew seller to continue loaning them. He was evidently surprised that I had visited at a time the whole village knew I was back in school. I took him through my reasons for being there, and requested his input into how I would manage the crisis.

His initial wish was to give me the money and send me back the following morning, but the cash on him was for a client's spare part; therefore, not to be touched. He invited me to share his food as we put our minds together into a strategy that would make me quick money in the next two days. Our options were limited as it had to be a business in which my face was not seen, otherwise information would get to my parents that their son, who should be in boarding school, was roaming around the village like a ghoul.

I had made the mistake most prison escapees make— focusing on the escape without giving thought to what I would do once outside. Time wasted while trying to find a grip is how escapees usually get apprehended. A notable moment came just as we tucked in for the night: we could sell cigarettes at a funeral vigil. But where was the funeral? Voke said he had not heard of any villager dying in the recent past. However, he promised to be on the lookout the following day and see if something came up.

I handed him my remaining pocket money as capital for two dozen cigarettes. That was an enormous risk. If he bought the stock and we could not find a funeral, all my money would now be in the form of cigarettes, a commodity I could not carry to school.

Voke left for work that morning reiterating that we needed to go to a funeral that night, even if it rained cats and dogs. I understood he was also afraid for himself by virtue of housing a runaway student yet he could not send me away since we had been through a lot together. My boy came back that evening with both cigarettes and great news. Seven kilometres away in the next village, a renowned teacher had passed on and would be buried in two days. Those were two nights of vigil for me and at a location I was assured of large crowds, since teachers had a strong union whose members stood by each other, though I risked bumping into Mom's colleagues who by extension knew me. I had learned in commerce class that entrepreneurs do not focus on the risk, rather, like an eagle, they use the raging winds to gain lift, and soar to heights ordinary birds such as chicken only dream of.

Voke went to his parents' house and brought supper on his way back, which we shared before heading out to our night business. I was dressed in his striped brown blazer, a pair of his oversized jeans that threatened to fall off, and a red dew rug I had carried with me from school. I looked like a thug. But then funeral vigils in my village thrive on such shady characters, since there is sale of the illicit brew, marijuana, and orgies in the bushes. Therefore, you cannot go there sheepish and expect to make a sale to people high on hard drugs.

At funeral vigils, it gets chilly at some point in the night and that's where cigarettes come in; smokers believe that puffing warms them up. The cold coupled with the craving and no alternative source means that at that hour they do not mind the cost, and you can sell at double retail price and smokers will still buy.

I had sold about eight packs out of the first dozen when someone walked up to us with searching eyes. He was none other than Mr Indimuli, a teacher at Mom's school.

"You are Madam Jane's son, right?" He asked.

I shook my head to signal NO, trying to keep my mouth shut. My voice, which was now full of rage, would have betrayed me. He extended his hand as if to pull off the dew rug from my head for confirmation. That persistence prompted Voke to swing into action in the nick of time. He clenched his fist and knocked the nincompoop's face so hard that he lost balance and tumbled to the ground. He grunted like a pig being choked to death. Voke and I burst out laughing as we took to our heels. We dashed back to the house feeling schadenfreude. That had been a brutal act, but a funny way to teach someone how to mind their business. I applied *Deep Heat* on Voke's swollen hand, thankful that the initial capital was back the first night. We would try again the following night.

Being the eve of the burial, there were more attendees; therefore, our sales increased and my merchandise was sold out before midnight. We did not see the curious teacher this time; I guess he was still nursing a stiff neck, broken jaw, or both. But I was sure he had not died, otherwise news would have spread the same day. On arrival at Voke's house, I took a nap and woke up at 4 a.m. the following morning to find my way back to school.

I walked the same route I had used when exiting. I passed the church door again, and then jumped back into the school compound. Luckily, my shirt was still where I had buried it, but it was damp from the night's dew. My whole body trembled on wearing it. Now, as long as I could walk all the way to my class for the morning preps, I was safe. Within eight minutes, I had managed to join my colleagues in class, half of whom were rubbing eyes full of sleep.

At my desk that morning, I took stock of how everything had gone from planning, to execution, to how I had fitted back in, and then it occurred to me that the risk had been worth it. In my wallet was more than twice the amount I had sneaked out with. Although it was not enough to pay for the shoes, it made for a substantial down payment. That was the type of return on investment blue chip companies are made of. I decided from that day henceforth, I would *jomp* and do business at vigils until I cleared Yobra's debt.

The problem with getting into such a vice is that it becomes addictive, and then one starts to feel invincible. It gave me an insight into why big-time robbers never carry out one big money heist, invest the stolen money and ditch crime to live in peace. Once your first mission succeeds, you keep going back—the experience and boldness on every venture washes away any thought of risk from your mind.

What had started as a transient exercise to repay the mutilated shoes became an obsession, a butterfly effect that made me jump over the school's fence to go party, drink, or watch porn. A pair of leased shoes altered the good student I had tried to be for a while, now I was addicted to walking a dangerous path. The good news is that I sneaked undetected for three quarters of my remaining years at Akili. The bad news is that it started affecting my concentration in class so much that my grades dropped drastically.

RUSTING

ALL THE WAY FROM THE main gate to the dormitories, Akili High School's surroundings are green; with tall trees lining up on both sides of the walkways, the neatly mowed green grass giving it a splendid ambience. With the forest cover around the compound so dense, you cannot convince anyone that the area suffers perennial water shortages.

There were water tanks attached to every building with a corrugated iron roof; classrooms, dormitories, dining hall and laboratories, but they were empty year in year out. Moreover, half of those tanks were not serviceable. Since the tanks were old, the gutters had clogged over the years and no longer collected rainwater. They were what Biologists call vestigial; as useless as the wings on chicken.

Teachers had the advantage of having plastic tanks at

the staff quarters. They also received a hardship allowance to buy from the vendors who sold water on handcarts. You could count the number of times our taps ran in a year, thanks to the jolly good fellows at the local water supply company. From time to time, someone in the company would be touched to open the taps for us, mostly deep in the night, and then we would be caught off-guard. We would run like headless chicken in search of vessels for drawing the water before it was turned off.

This mostly happened when someone higher up the echelons of government was expected to tour Kisumu and people had to be seen doing what government paid them to do. The status quo would be reinstated the following day. It is a cancer bedevilling Africa where we only do the right thing since someone is watching. We run red lights if there's no traffic cop in sight, or buckle our seat belts to avoid arrest.

There were seasons rain fell torrentially and filled all the tanks, but they would be empty again within a very short time. Rains would disrupt normal learning as we all got excited like young boys riding a new bike. The petrichor wafted into the air turning us into something else. With torrents pounding the roof and excitement getting the better of us, it was impossible to contain us in class, so we would run up and about shouting like possessed people. We had to have fun while it lasted before we were reset to default setting. Default, in our lingo, was rusting.

According to the dictionary, rusting is being affected by rust. Well, that description was not very far from how a standard Akili student looked during those months of lack. Since the school uniform shirt was white, the lack of water made it change over time. You wore the same shirt from Monday to Friday, without taking a shower or doing laundry. The collar would turn grey, then brown, then black; by Friday evening it had taken on a non-existent shade on the colour chart.

Why did we wear the same shirt the whole week yet we were admitted with two pairs of shirts? Every Saturday there was cleanliness inspection—everyone was expected to look clean regardless of the water shortage, otherwise you lost your dormitory marks and got into trouble with mates. For washing during the dry season, you got two cups of water; one for removing dirt and the other for rinsing. Therefore, we would form washing groups where we pooled the water together and washed as a group. Consequently, the once white shirts turned cream with time.

Nonetheless, for the savvy ones, the situation presented a business opportunity. One student collected as many white collars as he could and used the two cups of water he got to wash them. A collar is small in size, so the water offered was enough to wash and rinse up to ten of those, which would be dried then leased at five shillings on Mondays and Fridays, when hygiene checks were conducted. The leased collar would be pinned on top of the dirty one, and you put on a pullover to cover the rest of the dirty shirt.

Forget about shirts, those who were into sports wore the same pair of socks over and over. At some point, the fabric would break like a piece of crisps. Our noses adapted to the stench after enduring it for days in the dormitories.

Life was easier for prefects because they could access water from the kitchen. The rest of us had French baths, where you only washed the face, wiped the body with a damp cloth, and imagined you had showered.

Skunks stink? Oh please, we stunk like rained-on wild pigs in the jungle, so much that your own stench made you question whether you were still alive. We had dark scales of dirt sheathing our skins. The weird bit about it is that we got so used to each other that the smell never bothered us. The good thing about this hardship was that it taught us survival skills no institution of higher learning can offer.

Njiru, the school's old navy-blue Chevrolet pickup was the beast of burden that ferried water from reservoirs and rivers around for our use. It was named after one of Kenya's most celebrated rally drivers, Patrick Njiru. For a pick-up imported into the country by missionaries in the 60s, it was a hog in its twilight years headed for the death bed. She had outlived her productive years, so there were days she woke up with mood swings and just refused to start. Other times she would go all the way downstream, pack drums full of water, and then fail to raise enough horsepower to carry the load back. When Njiru broke down, which happened very often, we had to physically take our dirty selves and linen to the river, drink, wash, shower, and then carry some for use the following day.

Our school did not own that river, so we had to jostle over water with villagers who viewed us as intruders. The river is in a Nandi territory, who are traditionally herders, so sometimes the bone of contention would be over cows not being allowed to drink water peacefully. It was not a surprise to come back from your bush bath and meet a long-horned bull chewing the white shirt you had spread out to dry. Sometimes you squatted to shower only to see your bar of soap being gnawed by a nimble goat.

This set up also offered a robust opportunity to explore the size of each other's male appendage, giving respect to the *hangsome,* and laughing hysterically at the pea-sized ones. The defending champion for size was called Nzuki. It was rumoured that he carried so much weight between his thighs that his member swept the ground whenever he squatted to scoop water from a trough. He was respected on that front, and was nicknamed *Anaconda*.

Going to the river, especially on Fridays, was form one's forte because they were expected to submit a trough of water to the dormitory captain for cleaning the next day. Failure attracted a thorough beating, followed by punishments like being asked to go out and bring a bag of darkness, or calling your mother using a shoe as the handset to inform her how boarding school is dull, or coiling your body into a trough and sleeping there the whole night.

Those Friday evenings still traumatize me today. Sometimes you could not get water however much you tried. One option, for those who did not want to go to the river, was to steal from other students. This was considered legal as long as the owner did not catch you in the act. The phony way out was to play hide and seek until the captain slept, then sneak into the dormitory after lights went out. This was not a sure way either because dorms were locked from the inside; it was a fat chance you would get locked outside.

The second term was the longest in the school calendar, a time of a long dry spell when the sun shone bright until 6 p.m., fierce and scorching. Even the usually lush green grass took a beating this time, taking on a light shade of brown. This time, water shortage was worse, and the river was not an option since it was drying too, which meant continuous fighting with the villagers.

For the first time, I opened my eyes to what Global Warming really meant. I was comfortable rusting, since everyone else was just as dirty. Then, Mom decided to pay me a surprise visit. Had I anticipated the visit, I would have leased a collar or stolen a prefect's shirt to look presentable, but then she found the real me. I had pushed rusting to the extremes that day. The shoes were dusty, shirt was brown, pullover was no longer navy blue, and the trouser had patches of dust. I looked like a gravedigger just finishing off the task; and, being mid-month, I was penniless, hungry and emaciated. Veins popped out of my face like contours on a map, hair grown into an unkempt afro.

Mom walked past without recognizing me, went to sit on the waiting bench, and started looking around for someone to send in search of me. I followed quickly, heart racing, and called out "Mom!" She turned around and looked at me as though I had sprout antennae since she last saw me. From her facial expression, I could tell that her heart sank to a sinking low.

"Hillary, what is happening?"

"Nothing, what makes you wonder?"

"You look like a lunatic."

"I'm fine, Mom, just leave me alone."

"Stop telling me you are okay, and yet you resemble the school gardener. Are you dying?"

Mom did not want to be seen with me. She went to the teacher on duty and asked for permission on my behalf to accompany her home for the weekend. She took me to Tropicana Hotel in Kiboswa. I feasted on a full fish and vegetables, followed by a bottle of freezing cold soda. I ate and drank in silence, only nodding to the things she was saying. She inquired if I would accept a transfer to Mbale High School, as it was near our home, but I refused. I had become too accustomed to Akili way of life that grooming and becoming thin did not bother me anymore. I was fine as long as I ate and slept; the rest were unnecessary luxuries.

God must have intervened through Mom to get me out

of school that weekend. As fate would have it, there was an outbreak in what was suspected to be food poisoning ingested from the day's supper. I would have consumed that same beef had I been there. Students missed classes in numbers, the school infirmary bursting at the seams as more students reported for treatment that the medication ran out.

The school nurse seemed at odds of what do do. The rule was that you had to be seriously ill to be granted a leave out for further treatment at home. The rules were tightened as a stop gap measure of students pretending to be sick to take a break from school. However, even with all the stringent rules, there existed students who were perennially 'sick', spending a third of every term bothering the nurse for medication than studying. You would know their pocket money had run out the moment they complained of migraines and started missing a lesson, then two, then the whole day. Some simply chose to make it a den as they, for whatever reason, hated the school.

The other reason for minimized leave outs was that the school did not want to appear inadequate in medical provision to students. Plan B was usually a private hospital that shared one side of the fence with our school. However, the administration did not like taking students there because it had been established that most students, who were referred there, were not genuinely sick.

The thing is the doctor who ran the facility had teenage daughters, thus having them close to boys their age was a recipe for disaster. But relationships between his daughters and students was not even the doctor's biggest worry—he was more concerned with the fact that his girls would steal food meant for patients and pass it on to their boyfriends across the fence at night. This scheme was unearthed when, for the first time, the ever-lucky Atom was nabbed receiving a plate of chapatti and beef stew from Nancy, his girlfriend. I remember not only how Bokassa called him out during the assembly that morning, but his speech as well:

"I want to ask a young man in Form Two Blue called Nashon to step forward."

Atom walked into the middle of the curved assembly.

"Kneel down," he barked at Atom. "Ladies and gentlemen, this young man has been going over to that fence to receive food stolen from the sick, because he befriended a girl at that clinic. Nashon, you think by dating a doctor's daughter you will become a doctor?"

We all burst out laughing.

"Mister Deputy, suspend this young man today. Akili is not a place where we breed thieves."

The events of that morning marked the end of two relationships; one between the school and the clinic, and the other between my colleagues and their girlfriends. Atom would sadly carry the burden for all his accomplices in the scandal, thanks to the code of silence we all lived by.

Plan C was Jaramogi Oginga Odinga Referral Hospital in Kisumu, popularly known as Russia, but that too was not embraced by parents. Some had their preferred facilities and transferring a patient from there to your institution of choice was too bureaucratic. The school nurse was left with one choice: offer drugs, prescribe a different dose, try even others he was not sure about, and frustrate efforts to seek leave out. Whatever ailment was in your body would eventually die off, and then you would be healed IN JESUS' NAME.

This particular ailment was adamant, and the more the nurse offered treatment, the higher the numbers he received. Preliminary results seemed to tie the outbreak to our wanting hygiene, both personal and public. The rusting we comfortably lived with for years had seemingly taken a new dimension, albeit a scary one, but it became a critical learning point for the school administration. Sometimes, however, it takes tragedy for things to get better.

While the nurse continued working round the clock to find the best medication to whatever was ailing his patients, one student felt that he had been sick and patient long enough. He made the unpopular decision of going home without a medical leave out. The boy went to his box, packed a few odds and ends then walked out through the main gate after telling off the guards manning it. The issue was reported to the administration, the culprit identified and a suspension letter drafted to be picked the day he came back. He never returned. The young man got home, was rushed to hospital, but died upon reaching there.

The death could easily have been caused by something else and only aggravated by the illness, but then in times of crisis people stick to that which they believe in. It is the same way you get into a seemingly harmless squabble with someone unaware that he has a heart problem. The argument escalates and you throw a punch, just one, which sends him on a downward trajectory that eventually leads to his death. Like that, the tag of murderer follows you henceforth, with poor you behind bars.

His story lit a raging wave of anger in the student community, prompting the school to issue leave out chits to anyone who went to the infirmary regardless of mild, severe, or pretentious symptoms. It also shone light on a department that had for long been left to the doldrums, forcing a complete overhaul. A second nurse was added to the team, medical supplies increased, and the place was painted white. They even put a ceiling to cushion the place from direct heat from the roof. Blood tests, which had not been conducted since its establishment, became mandatory for students who checked in there.

The parents to the deceased boy did what Africans love—they brought the body to school for last respects from the community he had been with in his twilight days. In what remains the most emotional gathering I had attended at Akili, the usually verbose and tough talking Bokassa was short of words. His speech was short and slurred, occasionally taking breaks to wipe the free-flowing tears with his handkerchief. I had never known the old man could break down like he did that day. It hit me that those were tears of a parent empathizing with fellow parents who had lost a child. He was devastated.

COUP DE FOUDRE

High School Is A Time when students are between thirteen and seventeen; the prime of teenage years. It is a time when bodies, voices and minds are experiencing drastic changes. Pockets of hair dotted chests, beards sprouted, wet dreams happened, and lust kicked in. There were rumours the yucky taste of kerosene in our food stemmed from the administration trying to clamp down on our would-be runaway sexual urges. I didn't know that kerosene was a libido inhibitor.

Despite the kerosene therapy, we still lusted over skirts: the young librarian, female teachers—anything in skirts. We did not care about beauty, brain, and shape. We coined the phrase 'cover the face and storm the base,' then laughed about it like a pack of hyenas. Since the bulk of us were still virgins, we learnt about sex and everything that came with it from pornography or colleagues who had conquered such territory in their adventures. Those with girlfriends made fun of those who were yet to garner the courage to tune a girl. Sports and Science congress outings became the go-to events to hunt for girls. Some boys were bold enough to do it with ease and amassed women from different schools. Others, myself included, struggled with shyness and timidity.

After a series of unsuccessful trials, I decided to get into the industry through the back door. I even claimed a top seat at the table of men courtesy of my creativity and command of the Queen's language. I was the official love-letter scribe for fellow students, who had to maintain communication with their women but did not have the flowery romantic prowess and articulation.

Friday evenings, on the eve of an outing, were rush hour for me as instructions from different students sat on my desk waiting to be turned into mind-blowing letters for girls in different schools across the province. What I never understood was how I would write letters to several girls in the same school yet none wondered why all the boyfriends from Akili had a similar style and handwriting.

The only school I never wrote letters to was Bunyore Girls because their administration was strictly against boy-girl relationships. Actually, even talking to your own brother on an outing or receiving a letter was illegal. When Bunyore girls went on an outing, they would be locked in their bus to read or have group work. Only those participating in the events were allowed to go and represent the school. The restrictions paid since Bunyore girls were brains, churning out grade 'A' materials year in year out.

I would sit, put myself in the colleague's shoes, create

a mental picture of the recipient, and then write a *missive* to her heart sure she would giggle and blush. I would put my blood and sweat into those letters as though I was writing for my girl. The recipients replied in fine beautiful handwriting, letters that I had to read and reply as if I was the boyfriend. I was a conduit of love correspondence between high school sweethearts falling in love, so deep, yet I had no girlfriend to write to. I would buy pink writing pads and snow-white envelopes on every free walk, and then use them from the first to the last page, but everything would be words from my heart to other people's objects of affection.

Like a clingy mother who moves into her newly married son's house to keep an eye on the daughter-in-law, I became a third wheel in people's affairs. It pained me to witness a relationship grow to intimate levels, and then start crumbling. Nevertheless, I had to be the one reading and replying to the letters.

What most high school girlfriends those days did not know was that those young men they fell in love with were doing this for the first time, so many were as novice as they come. Yet they were expected to behave like the Mexican actors they watched on TV soap operas over the holidays. Jobless, broke and struggling fledglings were gauged against top actors who are remunerated to act romantic scenes, shed tears for love and take their women on paid-for dates.

As a frontline soldier in relationships, I can honestly say those boys were trying, it is the inexperience that bogged down some of them. They were exemplary because, in this side of the Sahara, fathers hardly take time to teach their sons some of these things. You are left to go head first into the murky world, disappoint a few unlucky babes, have a few sloppy frog-kisses, embarrass yourself and learn things the hard way. We grope through the dark, like a day-old puppy fumbling through a mound of fur in search of its mother's teats.

Few are lucky to get girlfriends with whom they grow and learn together while the rest frolic from woman to woman showcasing their mediocrity and earning a litany of names—one-minute man, bad kisser, or poor at romance, *et cetera*. These men, thus, grow up as big babies in matters of love and romance, and the world is not so kind to them.

Another easy way to die when it comes to romantic relationships is unrequited love. It is catastrophic. Regrettably, that happened to be the situation one of my platinum clients was in. I could tell that Vick was in love, for the first time. Well, as they say, the human brain functions well until you fall in love. The sort of love that blinds you from everything negative about your object of affection and only focuses on the tiniest shred of hope to cling on, even when your fingers are burning; the kind of love where one offers everything within and beyond their abilities and capabilities to make their eye-candy comfortable, sometimes giving away their own dignity.

Vick's girl was in a village school. He was into her, and he had money from his rich sister who ran a successful agribusiness around their home area. He tasked me with drafting letters to the girl every weekend, but she never replied. Communication is complete when the recipient communicates back; but when nothing is forthcoming you wonder whether the wording was too simplistic, too complex, or not worthy of a response.

In high school, two reasons made a girl fail to reply— she was too shallow to come up with a letter that matched yours or she was just not into you. I could tell Vick's was a case of sowing seeds on dry rock yet he insisted I include the line 'blue tears roll from my eyes as I think about you and hope to receive a reply.' He was of course lying about the bit of blue tears, but then he came out as someone desperate for love from the wrong person. Only true love can give one the zeal, energy and character to send out all those letters, receive none in reply and still have the willpower to write more.

The problem with girls, especially at that age, is they ignore chaps with honest feelings like Vick. They end up falling for playboys who hurt them beyond repair and forever live with the impression that men are heartbreakers. Nonetheless, I continued writing for him: he was a premium client, paid more for the premium writing pads and envelope, and at extra cost wrote the girl's name in ornate calligraphy.

I made five shillings on every letter but yet to fall in love to write my own. I was like a piggy bank hurled under the bed, holding all the notes and coins but not benefitting from a single shilling. There were times relationships died under my eyes despite all efforts to salvage things. The beautiful dedications I had borrowed from songs like Shania Twain's *Still the One* and Whitney Houston's *I Will Always Love You* to spice up their letters, would be replaced by Jojo's *Get Out*, *Wasn't Man Enough* by Toni Braxton, and Blue Cantrell's *Hit Em Up Style*.

The ripple effect of every broken relationship had two effects on me—loss on income and an unwilling amateur counsellor to a heartbroken client. I doubt Toni Braxton has the slightest idea how many relationships under my jurisdiction that *Unbreak my Heart* track saved. The experience I garnered later on taught me that the loss of first love shatters the heart to teensy-weensy pieces that you can never put together, and then I got to understand why some of my dumped clients toyed with suicide.

Nothing made me happier than writing a letter that salvaged an imminent break up. It made me feel like an invisible arbitrator who managed to read into two differing minds, picked something from each and joined them together. There were ambivalent nights when I would, on one hand, have a break-up letter, and on the other, a newfound love. The transitions between the two were not fluid, sometimes I had to take a break, walk to the washrooms then come back to a fresh page. Sometimes I became emotional, became part of the stories instead of remaining an objective outsider.

Being at the centre of all the love, I felt empty, and my heart craved for someone to love. That is as far as the good news go. When I developed feelings, it was for someone untouchable: none other than my History teacher whom I'll call Madam Blue. She was not only twenty plus years my senior but also married. For the three years she had taught me, I had never lusted over her; how things changed is still a mystery.

In my strange convoluted thinking, I imagined (even believed) she would leave her husband and come to me. She was a cleanliness freak who hated touching the chalk because the dust either dirtied her fingers or got embedded inside her sky blue acrylic nails. She dictated notes as written in the text book, only stopping at intervals to expound where she felt we did not understand.

Even with her wanton display of laziness, or attitude, history lessons became meaningful to me to the point that I would read ahead and participate in class discussions, something I never did with other subjects. Madam Blue would walk into class dressed in her signature flowing dresses, and my heart would melt. I admired the curls in her raven hair, or how her lips moved while she explained the Agrarian Revolution in Mesopotamia. Seeing that I was active in class, I became the go-to person whenever she posed a question and no one was willing to answer. Oh God, she was falling for me too, even with my oblong head!

My heart would flutter as I listened to her soft voice call "Lisimba," her eyes on me. I was in love. *So, this is how real love feels?* Aha, I could not wait to start writing her letters. At night I dreamt of Madam Blue, and I hoped she too was having the same dreams.

The sweetest dream of all was where we were taking a stroll on the shores of Lake Victoria, hand in hand. We were bare feet, exposing my crooked toes and her well-manicured sky blue acrylic toenails. Our feet left behind lovely imprints in the sand, like we were journeying through time leaving behind memories of our sweet life imprinted on the world. The sun was setting, lending the horizon a golden-brown ambience, perfect scenery for the picture-perfect photoshoot. I serenaded the woman of my dreams and complimented her smile, told her that she was beautiful.

Madam Blue suppressed a smile. I could tell from her blush that she really liked me. Her face had a rosiness to it; it was cute. Suddenly, I stopped, looked into her sleepy eyes and leaned over for a kiss. This was pure bliss *babba*, breath-taking. Blue shut her eyes and leaned closer for our lips to lock. And darn the devil, the kiss never was. Someone pulled my blanket, waking me up and denying me the chance to taste the lips of my desire. I cursed the senseless fiend for taking away the feeling that was coursing through me and left a wetness on my bed.

It was Mr Yellow-man who rudely interrupted my moment of pleasure. He stood beside my bed holding a hockey stick raised high up, a sign that any extra minute wasted in bed and it would fall on me. I bolted out of bed and ran outside in my boxers, leaving behind a deafening laughter from colleagues who were making a mockery of my roused throbbing manhood.

The dream doubled my feelings for Madam Blue. It was not just a dream, I convinced myself; it was a sign. Everything was so real that I could even smell her cologne around me. I was going to be more proactive in class and bring her closer, then one day she would fall in love with me and come to where she belonged. I requested for after-class lessons in her office and she agreed; at last things were going as planned.

One morning, while fantasising about her, I realised that her belly was slightly bulging. *No, she can't be pregnant.* My eyes squinted, zoomed in on that exact point, and the results did not inspire much confidence, so I concluded I was seeing my own things and let it go. However, the more the days moved faster than I wanted, the bigger the bulge grew.

Surely, how could she be this cold? Yours truly was an emotional wreck. This woman was going to kill me before my time. To make matters worse, the usually pleasant Blue, who stared into my eyes during lessons, stopped looking in my direction. It was as if she was trying to avoid me, and no matter how high I raised my hand, she never picked me to ask or answer her questions.

One day I was lost in my own world trying to unravel what I had done to deserve such scorn when she killed every ounce of hope in me. "Lisimba, why are you staring at me like that? Haven't you seen a pregnant woman before?"

Holy Mary mother of Jesus! I could not believe a woman this amazing had potential to spew such murderous venom. The whole class burst out laughing, and a lump blocked my throat. *She hates me, no doubt about that.*

I regretted not professing my love early enough, before she was put in the family way; maybe it would have slowed her down and wait for me. It was too late now. I had lost her even before she knew how I felt, the biggest loss in my then sixteen or so years on planet Earth. Even after being delivered of a bouncing baby girl, the relationship between Blue and me did not improve as I expected. She continued ignoring me and did not smile at anyone like before. Her after-class lessons were cancelled because she needed to go home early.

Moving on from my loss, I decided it was time to get myself a real girlfriend; one who was my age and not married. My heart was ripe for any girl that would give me a listening ear. A girlfriend I would call mine, kiss for real, take her on real beach walks, and write her love letters. I was intend on walking up to any girl and telling her what was on my mind.

The previous attempt had gone awfully wrong, when my words evaporated at the hour of need. In what may have been a spirited attempt to scorn me, the young girl had stood there waiting for me to say something. I scratched at a non-existent beard while my eyes darted from side to side. My tongue just refused to say anything, and the lady walked away, to the chagrin of a group of schoolmates nearby. Now, my resolve wouldn't have come at a better time; that coming weekend, there was Science congress.

On the eve of that congress, I *jomped* and spent the night in Kisumu bingeing on alcohol. I needed the alcohol-induced machismo to approach girls. Just like sneaking, alcohol had become a part of me that I often craved it whenever my mind was restless. I was plunging into addiction, bottle by bottle.

FIRST KISS

A TALL, LIGHT-COMPLEXIONED CHIQUITA swayed her hips from the far end of the compound across the field. She was in a white blouse, grey skirt, white stockings, and black shoes. The huge chunk of hair made her head look slightly bigger than normal, but hey, a bigger head could mean an expanded brain cavity, right? I could tell her face was accommodating, and if I did not grab this opportunity another would never knock on my door again. Finding a high school girl walking around alone was rare because most moved in groups like baboons. Thus, convincing one out of the pack meant dealing with a dissenting voice or two, which made things more difficult.

I approached her with gusto, head held high, but at an angle to hide the part that somehow was oblong. I extended my hand to break ice ...

"Hey, my name is Hillary."

"I am Kanaiza."

"Oh, that's nice. What a coincidence! My younger sister is called Kanaiza."

An introduction had never felt that simple, especially that I lied about my sister. She had chosen to give me her maiden name unlike the ratchets who relished English ones. I checked the badge on her blouse: OLIEL MIXED SECONDARY SCHOOL. I was finished. That was a school ten times below mine in the academic ranks, and one that Bokassa demeaned. During the previous year, their Social Ethics results were nullified for malpractice. Who even cheats in such a simple subject? Shouldn't they have copied a subject that makes more sense, like chemistry?

Coming to accept that Oliel in the local dialect means 'lit' was ironical. Another reason was that at the end of that same year, Bokassa had asked some form threes to repeat because their overall grades were way below the threshold for joining form four, but they refused. Their parents had instead transferred them to Oliel Secondary. Nonetheless, the same students considered academic dwarfs at Akili, had topped their first exam; thus, trouncing everyone else. According to Mr Bokassa:

"The headmaster of Oliel Secondary School phoned yesterday to thank me for giving him very bright boys. These are boys we sent away the other day, because they could not match up to our education standards. Now the headmaster is very proud that in this year's KCSE the school will have its first ever A or B."

Here I was making in-laws with an institution so disdained. The affair was an academic abomination. Kanaiza was in form one, way behind me, and even though she was here for the Science congress, there was very little science in her system. If that was the best her school could select to represent them, then Bokassa was right. While I thought I struggled in mathematics, the vivacious damsel was already doing worse in form one, yet she had made it on the list of Oliel's dream team on matters STEM. And that was not all: English was also not her cup of tea, contrary to yours truly in whose veins ran written words.

It then dawned on me that she had no qualms accepting my vibe because while it was a downgrade for me, for her having a boyfriend from the great Akili Boys High School was enviable by her schoolmates.

Kanaiza may have been a bit slow academically, but she was a good woman physically, behaviourally, and possessed most aspects that African men look for in a wife—polite, supportive, respectful, and beautiful. Thus , I decided to overlook the inequities and date her. It turned out our hawk-eyed Bokassa had spotted us together, and he was far from amused. Even though he did not mention my name, I was the subject of discussion during the assembly on Monday morning the following week.

"Have you people ever heard of anything called standards?"

I knew that was it. Bokassa was not known for throwing zingers out of the blues.

"Over the weekend, I saw one of you seducing a girl from this school down here instead of going for those Bunyore girls for a brain challenge. He wants one who is struggling so that he can chest thump with the Akili badge and feel accomplished."

With the snide or not, I was in love with Kanaiza and nothing was going to change that. Her school did not make it to the next stage of the congress, but it happened that one of the teachers in her school ran a side hustle in photography, so he was always found at school events. I leveraged on that connection to keep the communication lines open. The condition was that I had to keep promoting his business by taking unnecessary photos. I would also pay for him to take some of my blue-eyed dame and bring them to the next event.

Communication between Kanaiza and I was through word, thanks to our messenger, who would take my verbal message to her then come back with her response. After a short while, I remembered that one of the reasons I wanted a girlfriend was to have someone I could write letters to. One Friday evening, I wrote her a carefully worded letter, pouring out all the embers of love that had for years been muzzled in wait for the special one. There was the first draft, then the corrected draft, and then the correction of the corrected draft. Each subsequent one was an improvement of the previous.

It is from the third version that I wrote the final copy, taking everything slowly so that I do not ruin anything. The result was a masterpiece, arguably the best a high school boy had written his girlfriend that whole year. The perfection was close to what God must have looked at after creating Adam, before the idiot went around eating fruits offered by snakes. If I was a girl and received that exact letter, I would have fallen head over heels for whoever had written it. On the envelope, in calligraphy, I wrote: 'Zoom it to Car-Neigh-Zher, With Love.'

She replied, despite English not being her forte, on a sky-blue writing pad, sealed in a white envelope minus details of the addressee. After all the effort I had put in customizing her envelope, she had done absolutely nothing on the response. Such arrogance coming from a school like Oliel was appalling, but I still felt on top of the world. Her handwriting was big, with characters touching the base of every line on the writing pad, and then rising high up to hit the edge of the line above, like it was written for someone with poor eyesight. I went through it, once, twice, thrice, four times, and at the end of it all I could not understand what she was saying.

One line was that her heart had gone 'SANDYBODY OVER ME', whatever the hell that was. Instead of revelling in a beautiful reply from my freshly acquired high school sweetheart, I had a migraine from Akili High all the way to Timbuktu. Life has a weird sense of humour. I had always hoped for a woman I could exchange letters with like my clients, here I was in love with a girl who could not write a letter that made sense. I have to this day never fathomed what that girl intended for me to know, but I chose to stop further embarrassment by sticking to the initial word of mouth. I told our messenger to inform Kanaiza that I badly wanted her to kiss me over the holidays. I couldn't wait for my first kiss.

Butterflies flapped and fluttered in my stomach at the stage waiting for her. I was in a pair of maroon trousers, black and white sports shoes, African print shirt, and black cap that I wore facing backwards. For the first time in almost a decade, I applied Vaseline on my lips, the little jelly bottle still in my pocket in case I needed to add. She stepped off the *matatu* looking edible, like something headed for display. Her figure-hugging red dress with blue flowers clung to her body, accentuating the curves that her school uniform concealed.

The head still looked slightly big even with her hair

woven into banana lines, a fin-like protrusion at the back where all the twists met. She was here, mine for the taking. We spent a few hours strolling around the town until the sun set, reminding me that the day's biggest mission remained unfulfilled, yet Kanaiza was being slippery about it.

The murram road from Mbale town into my village is dotted with unfinished roadside constructions. In most instances, the owners did the foundation, raised the stone walls, but ran out of funds for roofing and windows, leaving the structures forlorn like a city recovering from the ruins of a civil war. Suffering years of desertion, most would grow weeds and shrubs that served as hideouts for children playing hide and seek, youths seeking to engage in illegalities like playing poker, and adults seeking some bush to pee.

I chose my location well; a neglected structure near a place called Oceanic by virtue of it being slightly farther from the main road. Even though we had a cloud of darkness covering us, Kanaiza insisted we hide in the depths of that building so that no one busted us, a new demand that was starting to annoy me. She must have noticed that my patience was running out and went into the stalled building first, while I remained outside to look left, right, then left again, like someone about to cross an eight-lane superhighway.

Sure the coast was clear, I stormed into the building like a rabid dog and edged closer to Kanaiza. I had waited a lifetime for this moment; the breath-taking minute for my lips to taste a woman's. Our lips reached for each other. If the eyes are the gateway to the soul, the lips are the same thing for the body. Her lips were soft, the promise of the sweetness to come. The feel of them sent my mind into a sensual state of intoxication, and I reached toward her face and held it in my hands. Electricity went through every nerve in my body. I was on cloud thirty-something. The kiss was short and long at the same time. Or maybe it never was. I only remember how I walked home with a bounce I've ever since struggled to replicate. I almost failed to eat supper that day not wishing for the taste of her lips to go away.

Back to school after that kissing holiday, something happened. Remember Shilla? The girl whose name was on both sides of Baron's mug? Good. The Barosh (Baron and Shilla) empire started crumpling. Shilla was bored. She wanted out. I got the sad news the day he asked me to write a letter expressing his hurt. He was angry that she was breaking up with him after spending all his pocket money and holiday tuition fees on her. 'I think that you have got another man, who has preyed on you like a hungry vulture. You are the love of my life!' I did my best to reconcile them, an avaricious arbiter who needed to protect his business. The battle was lost, taking away a good client.

The Barosh story has twists and turns though, like the movie *Shawshank Redemption*. Years later, I was at a petrol station fuelling my car when someone banged my window. I turned to give whoever it was a piece of my mind only to come face to face with none other than Baron.

"Hillary …" he shouted. I registered the wave of excitement in his voice. "Long time man, where did you disappear to?" He inquired.

He was in a neat cut navy blue suit, black and white tie, off white shirt and black belt. From inside the car I could not see the shoes. The side burns had been cut into a neat finish, highlighting the well-trimmed goatee on his chin. The lady in tow wore a mermaid-shaped African print dress, bringing out a figure eight curve. From her ears hung huge green earrings the size of a wall switch resting on her shoulders. Her head was shaven, with only a small patch dyed brown visible above the forehead. Baron was holding her hand tightly. They were behaving like a couple that just started dating; the man furiously guarding the clean-shaven beauty.

"Hillary, meet Shilla, my wife." He muttered, giving me a coded look to remind me about the letters.

That was the woman I had written letters to all those years! She looked calmer in person than the demands she had made a decade or so earlier. My jaw dropped on my car floor. *So, the high school sweethearts got past the teenage scandals and married?* Truly, emblazoning Shilla's name on his mug was the foundation to have it engraved in his heart, till death did them part. As a credit manager in a leading bank, he was doing well with his life, and wife. Shania Twain's *Forever and Always,* a dedication I had included countless times in people's letters, reverberated through my mind. Apparently, the lyrics had given Baron a beautiful wife. The two looked happy together, my little project.

I felt the pride of a potter looking at a piece of ceramic he had melded. The thing that tore my heart into two was that I was meeting the lady for the very first time in over a decade. Baron had not even thought of sending me a wedding invite to partake in the joyous celebration of a journey we started together. Out of all the relationships I had built, and overworked my pen to keep afloat in high school, this was the only one that I was discovering had withstood the test of time. The rest ended in tears with most of them disintegrating before we even got to form four, but whether they got back together, I have never known.

Even after ploughing my emotions into Kanaiza, I was not spared either. She dumped me in my first week of being a candidate; by word of mouth, through our messenger.

NIMBLE TOWN

OUR SCHOOL BOUGHT NEWSPAPERS DAILY for the library; however, we scrambled for two; *The Standard* on Friday, and the *Sunday Nation*. Friday was for the pull-out called *Pulse* and Sunday for 'Whispers with Wahome Mutahi', a humorous column that by extension is responsible for my desire to write. The two newspapers were hotcakes; they went missing faster than the speed of light.

For the rest of the week, we fed off an in-house vibrant showbiz scene sustained by rumours, counter-rumours, conspiracy theories, and propaganda. A week could not pass without drama from students, teachers, and the support staff. The school magazine was never short of the shady stories that brought levity to our rather boring lives.

First, scattered across the school compound were

monkeys, young and old. I always felt that it was us who had encroached on their territory and they only tolerated us. They loved visiting us in the evenings during games time; I guess they too had realized there was enough company from us, their cousins. They treated us their best and worst: they would rush into the field when a match was going on and take off with the ball and, other days, they stormed the kitchen and carted away whatever was lying around unguarded.

More often, they got impatient of waiting and dropped by earlier than their usual time. We would be in class struggling to stay awake when a monkey would chatter outside the classroom, jump in through the window, and storm out through the door. It often looked like they did this because they could get away with it. Other times, they would behave civilized by sitting quietly at the window and following the lessons like good students. The school should have made them pay fees for they attended many lessons.

On the other hand, there were rumours of ghosts roaming the toilets behind Menegai House. We did not know why Akili would have ghosts, but stories abound that the student who had died earlier after the food poisoning scandal had come back to haunt the school. No one had actually seen the ghost, but the narrative was convincing. Whoever started the rumour claimed that he had gone out at night to pee and a white humanlike hologram approached him with claws drawn.

The counter theory was that the space behind the said toilets was a smoking zone for some students, so they came up with the rumour to keep off snooping eyes when they discovered that the administration was closing in on them. When a few students braved themselves to sit out one night and meet this ghost, the narrative changed to that one of the new students in the same Menengai House was a night runner. There were graphic details of how he puffed up at night like a cat before disappearing from the bed.

One case was not a rumor, though, that my desk-mate, Simon shortened 'Symo', suffered from cerebral malaria. Simon was not only a good guy by all standards, but also an average student. On days the attacks took a sabbatical, he scored two marks out of a hundred in mathematics and zero in mole concept, just like the rest of us. But then, there were days his condition reared an ugly head and Simon lost it. Most of us were new to the concept of cerebral malaria, so the closest conclusion was that he was an occasional lunatic.

There were days when that demon bogged Symo down to a point of having conversations with himself. Most of these occurrences were manageable, and he would be issued a leave out to seek treatment as soon as his monologues were reported. However, we were yet to see the extent to which the disease had the potential to damage this young man with a promising future.

It was Saturday evening and the whole school was preparing for entertainment. Symo had been acting up during the day, but having been accustomed to his antics, we all disregarded it. When he was preparing to head for the entertainment hall, a fellow student made some remarks that annoyed him, and Symo snapped. Like a dormant volcano that had decided to erupt, while bubbling, Symo pulled out a penknife from his box and stabbed the guy. Those who were close by rushed to calm him down believing that he just needed to breath in and out for a few minutes then stabilize. They were not only flat wrong, but they had also underestimated his power. Symo wrestled his way out of the grip, and ran after everyone in the vicinity threatening to stab them. Since we could see his first culprit was proof, he could easily do it again; everyone kept a safe distance. His closest friends were asked to prevail upon him to hand over the knife and go home, but on this particular occasion interventions aggravated the situation.

"You want me to surrender the knife so that I get killed?" He retorted angrily.

I had never before seen such heightened paranoia in my desk-mate. This was a completely different individual from the Symo I knew, his eyes big red portent round balls. He was an animal, a gorilla. He was even chewing the collars on his uniform. He went gaga one more time and approached someone else in the group surrounding him, prompting a few courageous ones to brave the imminent danger and subdue him to the ground.

He was so strong that it took more than five boys to hold him down while one of the prefects rushed to call the teacher on duty. Or maybe he was not very strong, but rather people were just malnourished. It was too late to call his parents, and since he was deemed too dangerous to share a dormitory with fellow students, they locked him in the deputy's office for the night, hands tied with a rope to stop him from hurting himself. Symo's father picked him up the following day for medication and, a fortnight later, he was back, sane, fresh and fit as a fiddle.

What I learnt from that incidence is that humans only look decent as our brains work well; otherwise anything that upsets the balance can turn everything upside down in a very short period. You are better off ailing any other part of the body, but not the brain.

Hardly a week passed after Symo's return when we

were treated to yet another piece of entertainment from an unlikely source—the strictest and harshest teacher, Mr Ogetto. Life was difficult whenever he was on duty. Mr Ogetto wanted everyone on toes, hopping around like a rabbit. Whenever he was on duty, he criminalized strolling and hid behind buildings or trees then sprung on you out of nowhere, catching you in the act.

It happened that this time his week coincided with a time the skies had opened on Akili and the rains were pounding mercilessly. Since it rained countable times every year, the drainage system was not maintained. Whenever it rained, the channels got overwhelmed and broke to flood the pavements. Add the mud spread all over the pavements by over five hundred pairs of shoes and you can picture the crud.

Despite being the running week, we decided it was safe to walk, glossing carefully over the heaps of mud and pools of water. Mr Ogetto came out of the staffroom with a whip and started lashing at anyone walking, but then karma is a bitch. He was running after one of us with a whip when we saw him slide *vrrrrrr!* Off the pavement onto the grass, rolled several times then sat down *kutuuu!* Long skid marks dotted his journey to the great fall. When he stood up, his bottoms were all wet, like someone who had sat in a trough full of dirty water. It was clear he was not physically hurt, but his ego had got a beating.

We are taught to be empathetic when something like this happens, but it was funny. For us it was a treat, humour in gloom. Try as I may, I couldn't contain myself in. I burst out and laughed until tears flowed down my face. That marked the beginning of a reign of terror for me from Mr Ogetto. He did not teach me any subject, but he ended up beating me more than any other teacher in Akili, especially whenever he was on duty.

Short of in-house drama, grapevine and laughter, the school entertainment department did. It was a time so many changes were happening in the showbiz industry in the country; video data was moving from Video Home System (VHS), consumer-level analog video recording on tape cassettes, to Video Compact Disc (VCD). Audio was going digital for the disc man, and the Kenyan Hip Hop scene had just been birthed together with an FM radio station called *Kiss 100*. Most of the VCDs held movies released by then seminal Nollywood. I still remember the first ever Nollywood film I watched was about a woman doing all sorts of witchcraft, to stop the son from marrying a woman she disliked. She even went to the extent of capturing him in a little transparent bottle, so that he remained under her spell. The suffering portrayed in that movie was so massive that we, great men of Akili, broke down and filled the entertainment hall with painful tears.

An upgrade from the old stereo to a 3-CD changer also exposed those of us from the village to the digital world. It was mind-blowing to imagine that a machine could automatically select the disc and play the song you selected without rewinding or forwarding. Man, that was quite something, not the *Disco Matanga* style where we rewound tapes manually with a pen. Jack, the entertainment prefect, loved Ragga music and musicians Shaggy, Sean Paul, and Mr Vegas were the bulk of what we listened to. That was torture for people like me who had grown up on Reggae, because we had to harangue him to play Culture, Lucky Dube, or Morgan Heritage.

There was, however, one genre of music we all seemed to agree on—local music made in Kenya, by Kenyans for Kenyans. It resonated with everyone and the lyrics were in

Swahili. The content was fresh, the artists were young, and the rhythm upbeat. E-Sir, Nameless, Ukoo Flani, Jua Cali, Amani, and Wahu became the new household names, a breath of fresh air from the Maroon Commandos, Tshala Muana, and Yondo Sisters we had listened to since childhood. E-Sir would die in a grisly road accident not so long after, but his mark on the music scene was indelible.

The gospel scene too was not left behind as hymns by Emali Town Choir, Munishi, and The Omindes was replaced by the likes of Rufftone, Esther Wahome, and Henrie Mutuku. Gospel was taking a new direction, from liberal lyrics and hip dance moves to open displays of extravagance, an art perfected by the Congolese pop group Makoma. Those artists were way ahead of time, and the energy in their videos gave them this cool look we all envied. Their hit song, *Napesi,* brought me so close to accepting 'salvation', with 'saved', never mind that it was sung in Lingala and I did not understand a word. It hit nerves in my soul that no church hymn had done before.

This crop of young artists, who had taken the scene by storm, became an inspiration, showing that it was possible to follow your talent in the arts and make a name out of it. They were the success stories in a regime that had for long muzzled anything out of academics.

THE PALITO

THE CRAVING FOR MUSIC CREATED a demand for portable radios. The one in the market was a little transistor radio famously called the Palito. It could fit in your palm, with earphones that could be rolled into a ball and stashed in the pocket without being noticed. We listened to it under the blankets without being discovered. Like any contraband, being found in possession of Palito, yours or borrowed, was an offence punishable by suspension and hard labour when you returned. The damn thing would then be confiscated and locked in a drawer in the deputy headteacher's office, which was the storage for contraband waiting to be tabled as evidence before the disciplinary hearing.

Palito was addictive. You would be suspended, lose the gadget, yet go to the shop and get a replacement.

The adventure was in knowing you possessed something illegal and had to play catch-me-if-you-can with the administration. It kept your mind active as you were always trying to be a step ahead of FS. This included reading the mood of the administration early enough to anticipate an impromptu search and seizure operation.

Those swoops caught many by surprise, among them my friend SQR. His real name was Otanga. The nickname was borne out of the fact that he was short, quiet, and the proper definition of renegade. SQR was another rich kid; born with a silver spoon in his mouth, raised like a golden egg, and given everything on a platter. He was fond of telling us that we should not copy him because his future was as guaranteed as death is to living things. He was only at Akili to add a certificate to his name, but he really did not need the education. You would not expect any other reasoning from a son of an oil magnate.

His folks changed cars like clothes. Sometimes he would join us in admiring a beastly SUV parked in the administration's parking lot only for his old man to roll down one of the tinted windows and call his name. SQR had photos of his elder brothers and sisters in the United States, the only thing separating him and joining them being a high school certificate. He bribed the class prefect to never rut him over mistakes, and always paid the geniuses in our class to do assignments then let him copy. He may have been reckless, but when it came to anything that would jeopardize his successful completion of school, he freaked out big time.

That is how I found myself in discussions with him over the risky plan. It was of sneaking into the deputy's office to steal his confiscated Palito among other contrabands. His disciplinary case was coming up in a few weeks. The only way to save his soul from an impending expulsion was destroying the several pieces of evidence stacked up against him, the stereo being one. The boy had done his reconnaissance and known the exact drawer the radios were kept in; now he was working on finding out whether or not the drawer was locked with a key. He offered me 600 shillings (6 dollars) for the job, a handsome figure if we pulled this off in the less than ten minutes he expected the operation to take. I had pushed fate to the limits before and got away with it, but the risk factor in this particular one was too high, so I turned down the proposal at first.

The experience taught me we all are proud when desperate; but when push comes to shove, we can easily engage in the very things we swore against when it comes to survival. That is why there exist graduates doing menial jobs to eke a living, as well as fine-looking lasses hawking confectionaries on busy highways.

Thus, I reconsidered my decision to turn down the offer. Someone stole my seat after the previous weekend's entertainment night. This was a common occurrence at Akili. I searched for it in all classrooms and there was no seat that looked anything close to mine, which meant the identification mark had already been erased and replaced with something else. It was a booming business where you contracted a thief to find you a replacement after losing or breaking yours. It would be their job to steal one, erase all identification marks and give it a new look to officially make it yours.

Efforts to keep my crime list low by asking for a replacement from the furniture store were in vain. This left me with the option of piling my books on top of each other to create something like a stool for me to sit on. The books were not so many, so I was unable to reach the writing surface on top of the locker. I would sit on the books when the teacher was speaking then stand up to write when he or she started dictating notes. It was too much trouble, so I needed money to buy a new chair from the black market. Suspension for breaking into the deputy's office would have been the reason my Dad's face would appear in news headlines for killing his son, but why would I care about his making headlines when I was dead?

It was about 7.30 p.m. when SQR motioned that FS was headed towards Form 1R, a window of opportunity to pull off our heist. What he had not mentioned was that he was paying me 600 shillings because I was the one to sneak into the office and make away with the Palito. According to him, he was already in bad books with the school, so being found in such an act again would have worsened the situation. In other words, it was my turn to taint my spotless reputation and earn a spot in the black book, for six hundred Kenya shillings.

I walked majestically into the administration block, like a student going for an appointment with his teacher, then went into the lounge, where teachers always sat over lunch or to catch up on gossip. I was doing that to confirm there was no other teacher in the building that night, lest I jumped from the frying pan into the fire. My stars had crossed, there was no teacher.

Flying Squad's office was on the ground floor, nestled in the farthest corner in the East Wing. From his office window he had the advantage of an expansive view of the football field stretching all the way to the bend that disappeared into the main road. His was the first window the sun rays ripped through every morning.

My blood raced as I docked outside the brown door with the words 'DEPUTY HEADTEACHER' carved into a black metallic plate. Behind that door was a tiny gadget that had a significant part to play in my SQR's fate. It also held the keys to me making a quick buck, paying someone to get me a seat, and going back to my usual life. I grabbed the latch and twisted it to the right, then gave the door a light nudge. It opened. Just like those moments I jumped across the fence, I was officially in harm's way, and any wrong move here would have seen me expelled even before the boy I was trying to help.

For a while, I stood at the door wondering whether to proceed or close it and forget about the whole idea. *Jomping* had, however, taught me that once you engage the first gear you have to move forward; hesitation is a waste of precious time, which you don't have the luxury. I walked in.

At the centre of the office sat a wide mahogany table with drawers on both sides, and a black swivel chair in the middle behind the desk. A black coat dangled from the backrest.

According to SQR's recce, the contraband was kept in the middle drawer to the left side of the table. I pulled it out and true to the young man's words, there were tens of things in that drawer: Palitos, packets of cigarettes, a Discman, condoms, rolls of what looked to me like Marijuana, and several pocket knives. You mean fellow students had the courage to bring in all these things, and here I was calling myself a top criminal for *jomping*? I consoled myself that mine were infractions and misdemeanours—I hurt no one, never did drugs, and did not threaten anyone's peace in the school. The fence I always jumped over remained intact, even after all those escapades. Furthermore, I sneaked to create an additional revenue stream that supplemented what my parents gave me, which could pass as entrepreneurship. With the look of things, Akili harboured criminals.

There was a problem though: SQR had not given me sufficient description of how to differentiate his Palito from the tens of others there. They all looked the same to me, save for the different numbers written on top with felt pen. I concluded that those figures indicated the case files on each one, a number both my client and I had not cared to find out. I was now in the deep end, looking for a needle in haystack. I was torn between picking the first one my hands landed on and going through the black counter book sitting on the table to find out SQR's case number. Picking any would have destroyed evidence yes, but to a case we both had no idea about. I took the risk and opened the counter book. Lines ran from top to bottom of the book, creating columns calibrated: Date, Name, Class, House, Case Number and Remarks. I read them:

Ken Murila / 3W / New Kenya / CN 146-01 / Participated in attempted strike – Expelled.

David Kirui, Nickname Rui/ 4G/ Longonot / CN 145-01 / Possession of 1 box of cigarettes – Suspended.

Rui was Akili slang for rude, and only the very hard-core merited that title. How coincidental it was that his parents had named him KI-RUI way before any of them knew he would live up to the name. It was honourable to be counted among those giving FS sleepless nights, as it meant you were essentially above civilian law, a privilege most of us wished for. Chills ran down my spine when my eyes fell on the third name, it almost ended the mission there and then:

Hillary Mbarani. 2R/ Elgon/ CN 147-01/ Sneaking suspect –
Under surveillance.

The English name was exactly mine, and the second
one (Mbarani) had a very close semblance to one of my
other names; Ambani. I read it quickly the first time that
is why I thought my name was already in the bad book.
Why, in heaven's name, did this namesake also sneak? He
was putting our name on the administration's radar for
no reason. A page held about twenty names, some cases
having more details than others, depending on the severity
and evidence. Where to begin searching for my client's
name was the challenge. He had also forgotten to inform
me, when his contraband was confiscated, so that I use
dates to guide me. One should never go into a larceny as
clueless as I was that night; I was confused on what to do.
I was still skimming through the names hoping to spot my
client's name, when I heard footsteps approaching outside.

GOONS IN BLAZERS

THE PERSON WHO INSTALLED THE lockable bookshelves in the deputy principal's office needs to be hailed from generation to generation. That's where I sought refuge. I had to spread my body against the back wall like a lizard for the door to close. There were piles of books pressing against me from all directions, their sharp edges poking into my flesh. I just needed to control my breathing and the pounding of my heart. I felt like my chest would burst out as the office door squeaked open. That was it; I resigned to the glaring fact that I was spending the night in my father's house ... or in a morgue.

Thoughts trundled through my mind: SQR had not played his watchdog role well, leaving me vulnerable. He had by now probably taken off, went back to his desk, and abandoned me to burn. But then, he was not to be blamed.

Choices have consequences, and I had knowingly pushed it; I was not supposed to cry foul. In law, it is *volentinon fit injuria*. I could already picture myself telling my old man that I had been caught stealing a radio from the deputy's office. Even I would *kill* my son if he was suspended for such misdemeanour. You would rather be caught stealing books, or chemicals in the laboratory. But stealing a radio, a contraband, from the deputy's office? My thoughts were interrupted by a slap falling on someone *paaaa!* It was FS slapping a student.

"Who gave you the authority to fight my prefect?" FS asked angrily.

Before the culprit answered, another slap followed *paaaa!*

"You fought him because he is in Form One and you are two classes ahead?" (*Paaaa!*)

"Are you aware that prefects hold my authority regardless of their age and class?" (*Paaaa!*)

Up until that moment, I had never known how claustrophobic I am. It was starting to get uncomfortable inside the book cabinet; it felt like I was in an incinerator awaiting cremation. I was really close to choking, a situation made worse by the fact that my body was tired of being in that awkward position for long. As I squirmed in there, my mind began preparing for the moment I would let go of the grip, and tumble out of that hideout.

As the minutes dragged, my muscles wore on, and the apprehension kept going in circles: FS reminding the culprit about respecting authority, the victim being a mono, and then FS meting out on the culprit the wrath of such crime. With the slaps checking in fast and furious, the young man started crying, apologising profusely. From what I gathered, a newly elected dormitory assistant had gotten into some disagreement with the culprit, who told him off on the basis of being younger. Feeling disrespected, the prefect followed the boy to his class and tried to slap him before his classmates.

As a matter of principle, a form one student cannot try that stunt on someone considered his elder in Akili. With all the weevils a form three had eaten from school beans and remained alive, what would give a mono the moral authority to strike him? The class booed the young man, fuelling resistance in their classmate that did not just end in him blocking the slap, but also disintegrated into a fight. In a school where prefects were sworn enemies to civilians, it took the deputy's intervention to save his young prefect from being beaten to pulp.

You see, the one mistake our administration made was vesting too much power on the prefects. To stand out, prefects wore badges and maroon blazers instead of navy blue pullovers like the rest of us. Each blazer had white, black, and gold stripes on the hands and pocket depending on seniority and department. Other luxuries they enjoyed were sleeping in little cubicles that every dormitory had and eating without having to queue, which made them live like assistant teachers. Most went the extra mile and picked servants, *monos*, whose jobs would be to keep their diary, follow through on pending issues, and ensure their outfits were always sparkling clean.

These service providers were introduced to other prefects, and the kitchen staff, so they would be allowed to collect food for their bosses to eat from the comfort of their cubicles. Being a 'servant' was another coveted position in Akili. In addition to eating the same food the masters ate, they were exempted from manual work because they were busy taking care of the 'big men.' That prefects had to look neat also meant the cubicles always had water, so servants would wash their own uniform alongside those of their masters. These stalwarts had to be loyal to their masters even to the point of snitching on their friends otherwise they would be dethroned and lost the privileges.

Losing the privileges meant isolation from peers because the prefects were known to be goons in blazers and loathed in equal measure. In Africa, it is said that the stick used to throw the millipede away is also tossed along with it.

The masters were, on the contrary, unappreciative to their servants. You would expect that the masters would recommended their servants for prefect positions when vacancies arose, but they never did so. This was to ensure they remained forever servants because, what would you expect of their relinquishing servitude? They would pick their own servants and they would be probably worse than their masters were.

By rule, the prefects were infallible. A case between a *peeree* and civilian always ended in favour of the former, because his word was final. Some prefects leveraged on this to make life difficult for those they did not like, and, consequently, they ended up being the most hated arm of the system. If it ever happened there was a murder in Akili, it would have been of that of a civilian killing a *peeree*. In all the entire foiled student strikes, there always existed an attempt to douse the prefects with petrol and set them ablaze.

Moreover, the prefects were law unto themselves. They enforced their laws through a stupid unofficial unit they started called DISCO (Disciplinary Committee). It happened every Friday night in the head-student's cubicle, where *peerees* would forward the names of those who had erred throughout the week. The culprits would then be flagellated by all prefects, in turns.

Every student on the prefect's A-List was guilty as charged in the DISCO court. And the administration was aware of DISCO and its machinations, a kind of an illegal entity operating under the auspices of the administration. It was more of a torture chamber sanctioned by the authorities. Akili wanted discipline by the hook or nook without even according the accused a fair hearing. However, the prefects did not know that when you rule with such an iron fist over fellow students with whom you share classrooms, pavements, and dormitories, you should be extra careful because the karma bitch is never far away.

One student, John, grabbed everyone's attention with his charisma, wisdom and quick decision making that he was primed to be the next Head Student. He had risen through the ranks quite exponentially, so fast that he forgot he too had joined Akili a humble naïve boy like the rest of us. He had focused on becoming the top guy and forgot why he had gone to school. Examinations do not recognise and respect authority. He was caught cheating in one of the papers, and though the teacher forgave him, word went around that the most revered boy was a low-life exam cheat.

The story spread like wildfire, and in the process unearthed a damaging secret about him—he was homosexual; he pestered young boys in his cube against their wish. In our society, homosexuality is not a word you utter anyhow. Thus, the issue was magnified, and five or so boys who had been his victims came out. As if that was not enough, there was a third allegation that he was the one behind the recent wave of theft which had led to disappearance of people's shoes from different dormitories.

The thing about rumours about a person in such a

position is that whatever is said is taken as the gospel truth, and there is absolutely nothing you can do to clear your name. It is even worse if friends turn enemies and witnesses against you because you were so drunk with power to the point of burning bridges. That evening, some boys waylaid Johnie-boy in the hallways and emptied a trough of dirty water on him, shouting "faggot!" He *jomped* that night, leaving behind all his belongings.

I was jolted out of my thoughts by the deputy shouting instructions to the boy he had been apprehending:

"Stand here, stretch your arms, and get hold of this table."

I knew the drill. That was the deputy's style of whipping lawbreakers. You stood at a distance, stretched yourself, and got hold of the table as if you were swimming in mid-air, and then angry strokes would fall on your bottoms. While in that position, you were not allowed to remove your hand from the table to massage the pain off where the strokes were landing, otherwise the stroke was considered void. In FS's judgment, the culprit's misbehaviour merited ten strokes of the cane. Therefore, the trick was to slip into vegetative state and only come back to life after the walloping was over. I could literally feel the pain as I listened to him cry, whips ravaging his buttocks.

When all was over, the deputy ordered that he goes to mop the dining hall alone, then come back for his suspension letter. In my unsolicited opinion, the punishment was overkill. I had seen worse crimes in the deputy's black book. But well, that's life: first time petty offenders are usually punished severely than hard-core crooks. I could tell the poor boy regretted being carried away by mob psychology to fight that mono, but then these moments of temporary insanity were common among students.

Most of our hearts harboured pain, rage, and hate, bolted like a top secret, so much that whenever an opportunity to let it out came, emotions overrode reason. We were like the Coward of the County that the late Kenny Rogers sung about, emptying our years of frustration on anyone unlucky to cross our paths. Most times, you would regret after the damage was done. I lost count of colleagues who were expelled due to moments of insanity. When they came back to their senses, no apologies or remorse swayed the authorities.

DEN OF FRUSTRATIONS

TEENAGE IS ALL ABOUT REBELLION, curiosity and attention seeking. What you do is looked at in the lenses of the society and peers. And when you go to a good secondary school, expectations are high. For students from backgrounds where the highest achievers did not go past primary school, a lot is expected; the entire village looking upon them to light the way for others. Others get funded by well-wishers to go to high school thus the pressure to perform is from different quarters who are interested in their beneficiary's performance. Then there is the majority from well-to-do families known to produce academicians; the bar already set high and you have to keep at par lest you be the one to disappoint the family and the society.

Additionally, there are challenges underlying any family, as there is no perfect society. Some students had frustrations from home, tagging along issues like parents being on the verge of divorce, or fights between siblings over property, or close family members with chronic sicknesses.

The school badge on the left side of your shirt where the heart is was a constant reminder that you had the best interests of the school at heart, Akili was a name worth not to be muddied by poor performance. Thus, despite teen horniness (which is not a crime to say the least), peer-pressure, societal expectations, and your own devils, you were expected to perform. Nevertheless, without proper guidance from teachers and parents, such an endeavour is an exercise in futility.

One of my letter writing services clients was battling depression. Over the holiday, he had tasted the forbidden fruit and word had it that the form two girl at Goibei Girls was pregnant. His parents were yet to know that they would soon be grandparents, but the heat from the girl's folks was already incinerating his life. The pregnancy had been discovered during the regular checks in the first week of opening school. The girl had been sent home, and the disappointed parents were pushing her to reveal the identity of the man responsible.

According to the most recent letter, the girl was giving them silent treatment, but threats of being thrown out of home were coming in their droves. This meant it was just a matter of time before she was bullied into revealing. Hell would soon break loose. I pictured their parents frog-marching them to the chief's office for a crisis meeting. That would mean my client would forget school, get married and start a family uneducated, unemployed and inexperienced, their dreams of a better future prematurely cut short.

Such are some of the issues some Akili boys carried in their hearts, wondering where to offload them. To vent off, during blackouts, they attacked prefects. Otherwise, it was not easy to sit the Guidance and Counselling master down, and tell him the issues gnawing on your insides thus affecting your performance. The department was resourced with all necessary materials and boasted a well-oiled team, but it failed to foster trust and seamless communication with the students, who felt disenfranchised from the same system.

The mistake was that counsellors branded themselves as a unit assembled for corrective surgery on misbehaving students. In other words, it was where the rogue went to be harangued back onto the right track. None of us ever saw it as a place to go if, and when, you had a problem bothering you.

This was compounded by the fact that, in Africa, men are not supposed to be emotional. Growing up, you are constantly told not to cry wolf like a woman. Men only cry in the rain, where the tears are washed away by the torrents. Stories abound of strong men who commit suicide and their suicide notes point to depression, but testimonies by their family, friends and relatives paint a picture of a jovial person whom they wonder what drove them to suicide. Many smiles are like a 3-ply mask meant to block the dark cloud inside from percolating onto the surface.

Scientists posit that one sign of depression is extreme anger, and the boy I witnessed being walloped by the deputy had all the makings of depression. His mistakes were not as serious according to me, but his retaliation painted a picture of an irritable teen. If you were unlucky to attract the authorities' attention for such a crime of beating a prefect, you would pay for the sins of all those who cheered you up and serve as a warning to future would-be offenders. Had the administration ever wondered why one or two prefects were always knocked out whenever the lights went off?

The young man was being thrashed, would be given hard labour as punishment, get suspended and be back after the two weeks to continue sharing the same environment with his nemesis. If he had harsh parents like mine, they too would run over him during his suspension period, adding salt to the injury. There would be no reconciliatory efforts initiated between the two to ensure they lived harmoniously after the episode. So the boy remained aggrieved and bitter, a lethal enemy to the *mono,* whose small trappings of power had, from the look of things, gotten into his head.

The prefects too should have been counselled to extend olive branches to those they ever punished or harassed when their time to exit was nigh. Very few, if any, ever did. Some students do leave high school still holding grudges against one or two prefects. At Akili, it was us against a savage system supported by parents, who most times believed the stringent rules were the gateway to academic excellence. When a school is reputed to produce top performers, parents tend to dump their children there, pay fees and wait to collect good grades. Whatever happens in between is left to the teachers, and as long as nobody dies the rest doesn't matter.

I listened as FS, the prefect, and the boy who had beaten the prefect walk out of the office, followed by an eerie silence. Even the crickets that had been stridulating outside were quiet. I felt like I had been caught up in a shootout between cops and thugs; then, abruptly, the guns went silent, leaving me with a pulsating heart. Whereas my body trembled from a sharp wave of cold, I was sweating ghastly like melting ice-cream. I listened to be sure that it was safe to crawl out of the book cabinet. The best practice in the books of Akili would have been to go back to the Black Book and complete the day's mission but I was not risking another minute in that office, after staring a suspension in the face. To hell with the money, I was going to class.

In the weeks that followed, SQR faced the disciplinary committee and was adjudged to be a thorn in the flesh. He had been suspended more than his fair share, but nothing seemed to make him better. His rap sheet boasted crimes like *jomping,* possession of contrabands, recalcitrance, and reckless behaviour. There was only one verdict—expulsion.

SQR was not the only one having a rough week, as the chickens finally came home to roost for my client whose girlfriend was pregnant. He was pulled out of the great Akili into a day school, where he would work on people's farms and herd cattle over the weekends to raise money for the baby.

That demotion in status was hard to take in as villagers started scorning him for being a failure. In essence, he was handling a myriad of: accepting the new low, learning to be a family man, watching his future waft into thin air, and being the laughing stock. It was too much for him to take, and word had it that he had decided to end his struggles, shame, and suffering. He was found hanging on a rope in someone's cowshed, and just like that the grave took in another genius, thanks to one adolescent mistake.

THE POISONED CHALICE

O F ALL MADNESS, AKILI BOYS High School had a
bus christened the name of a beer: Tusker. But why
wouldn't it when the vehicle was bought from a brewing
company, then repainted from yellow to white and blue? It
may have been old and jalopy-looking, but it commanded
equal respect for us since beggars are not choosers. It had
a knack for breaking down when most needed, as though
someone had cast a spell on it and died before lifting it.

On the few days Tusker woke up in good spirits, the
driver would kick 'start' and the whole area around it
became a cloud of thick grey smoke. If there ever was a Hall
of Shame for the largest contributors to global warming,
Tusker would hold top position. It had a long gear lever
sticking out of the gearbox, so rickety that everyone knew
when the driver engaged gears up or down. The engine

roared like an injured lion. The first gear was super heavy and peaked lazily, so the bus would drag itself out of the parking like a truant walking to school.

Save for the seats which were black, the interior was all white with a NO SMOKING sticker pasted on both sides of the cabin. Above the driver's seat was a red first aid box with a cross drawn over it. I never saw the box opened to know how stocked it was. We all trusted it the same way airline passengers have confidence in flight attendants when they say life jackets are under the seats. Tusker's seating capacity was something we never bothered to know; most students preferred to stand and enjoy the interesting views outside whenever travelling, otherwise to admire girls.

What made our relationship with Tusker bearable was that it managed to take us on school outings. However, making it on the list of those to go to such outings was as difficult as the Biblical camel passing through the eye of a needle. You had to be phenomenal in whatever item the school was sending you to represent since with ordinary reasons, you risked being struck off the list when the bus was leaving. We referred it as *kuachiwa moshi,* because Tusker would drive off and leave you covered in a cloud of smoke. One way to get aboard illegally was slipping in through the window, a popular choice for those who already suspected they would be dropped. Others would board earlier and squeeze under the seats, only to appear when the bus had hit the road.

The other alternative that guaranteed your position on the list was greasing the palms of students in charge with a few coins to include your name among those at the very top of the list, even if you had no role in whatever activity the rest were going to partake. The build-up and hype around school trips made *kuachiwa moshi* so embarrassing that it affected your esteem for the whole week. Actually, culprits did not go back to class as instructed; most detoured to the infirmiry and 'fell sick' until the heartbreak waned off.

Going on a trip began weeks in advance as representatives spent man-hours fine tuning their craft and rehearsing late into the night. There were rigorous processes, so tough that those initially interested dropped out voluntarily along the way, while the other third was eliminated on D-Day.

This was Jerry 'Manywele' Okaga's story. He was the typical don't-care *mono*, who looked more rugged than most seniors, with his dirty brownish shirts, faded trousers, and unpolished shoes. We became friends when both of us were trying to gain entry into the drama troupe. We were eliminated at the auditions because of weak vocals that couldn't earn the school a point at the festivals. To be honest, I knew even before attempting that I have a croaking voice heavy with Maragoli accent. I was only trying my luck at a school trip seeing how returnees from such were held in high regard, a spectacle of pandemonium for hours as letters from girls were delivered to the respective recipients. We would mill around them to listen as they narrated the day's highlights, scenes, and goofs.

I never went back to the music hall, not after the initial embarrassment, but Okaga had this resolve that unless God called him back home, he was representing the school in his *mono* year. He turned up with a hollow plastic pipe and huge pot, *inyingu*. No one knew where he got the items, but the moment he blew into his pot through the pipe, the choir master knew he had found a valuable addition to the year's presentation of traditional songs. Okaga had ingeniously carved out an indispensable role for himself because if they dropped him, he would leave with his pot. He henceforth became a permanent fixture on the troupe, blowing his lungs to the benefit of everyone. Character would soon cost him, and the school at large, a coveted place in the finals.

Then there was Michel 'Bata', a miniscule *mono* with a shrill loud voice. His toes were so close together and the feet appeared webbed, like a duck, thus the nickname. Bata gained quick entry into the Akili history books as having the most flexible waist the institution had seen in years. African men are not exactly blessed with bodies that can twirl and swirl, hence having him on the troupe was an arsenal that the traditional dance ensemble needed to stay ahead of competition. When the young man's knees kissed the ground, and waist took the form of a wasp, even the ever-busy Bokassa left his upstairs office to come watch him gyrate. It was like a little wonder that God had sent to Akili School. Efforts not to look at his feet and see the webs were futile.

The troupe was heading to the provincials when Manywele, in his true fashion, came to the bus looking like he had crawled out of a garbage bin. He looked like the day's onboard mechanic in case Tusker pulled one of her signature tantrums. The teacher in charge gave him one look and ordered him to find an outfit that looked more presentable. For an institution where water was like the proverbial blue moon, getting a clean shirt was no walk in the park, so he opted for what most students did when faced with laundry problems—*go shopping*.

This was the term used to describe the act of scouring through dormitories or washing areas in search of outfits that had been washed by the lucky few, who may have somehow conjured water. Form ones' outfits were most sought after, by virtue of them being new and white because those worn by the seniors were worn out or discoloured, which made stealing them a waste of time. In an institution with boys as huge as giants and others miniature like rabbits, going shopping required more time. You had to carefully select a perfect fit lest you stole something for no use.

The unwritten rule was that once you stole someone's outfit, you were to return it at the same spot as soon as you came back from the trip. Keeping it was considered a bad omen; that it increased your chances of being dropped on the next outing. Since most shopped garments were returned, we considered it leasing rather than stealing. Manywele took too much time searching for an outfit his size that the bus left him.

The national level entry was in such close proximity that the excitement blinded everyone from noticing Manywele was missing. It was only until our traditional dance troupe was called on stage that they realized there was no one to blow into the painted pot. Mistake two was that the troupe had over-practiced the previous night, making everyone so confident that they ignored the pre-stage rehearsal; otherwise they would have noticed Manwele was missing. Previous performances by this team had been electrifying, thanks to Manywele's magic pot and Bata's flexible waist.

When it was Akili's turn on stage, there was commotion as everyone sought a vantage position to catch a glimpse of the long-awaited masterpiece. It was an open secret that this troupe was bound for the national festivals, unless someone became greedy enough to sell off the result to a less deserving competitor. The troupe was in disarray for many dancers had depended on Manwele's pot to create symphony.

The eerie silence, reminiscent of a graveyard, said it all as a wave of disappointment descended upon the team. I was on this trip as the journalist on location, a path I had taken to gain backdoor access to outings without having to sing, swing my waist, or blow into pots. The good thing about being the journalist was that you were assured of both sports and academic outings, but the challenge was writing the story, especially when the school was eliminated.

Disgruntled voices pointed an accusing finger at the music teacher for asking Manywele to go change when everyone had accepted him as scruffy as he was. She became an instant enemy, like the biblical Moses leading the Israelites into the wilderness without food and water. The teacher made yet another unwarranted blunder—she ordered everyone to assemble and head back to school, since there was no use staying around. With a lot of time left to the official closing ceremony, and guys dying to go chase after skirts, a silent revolution erupted and everyone disappeared into the crowds.

For close to two hours, the teacher tried all she could to get her students aboard the bus in vain, despite the countless times it was announced on the PA system. She walked around rounding up the visible few and forcing them into Tusker, but then she would come back with a new lot and find the bus empty again. In the spirit of looking out for a brother, we would inform each other to avoid the direction she was headed. Threats of the bus leaving did not scare us, not even when Tusker's conspicuous black smoke could be seen bellowing into the skies. At some point she got tired of the cat and mouse game and made good her threat, asking the driver to leave with the few *monos* on board; a mere eight students out of the fifty-eight that had left school for the festival. That would become the lucky lot.

The rest of us were sure the bus would come back

for us, since our parents were billed every term for its maintenance and fuel. Not so long after Tusker leaving, the skies turned black and the heavens opened; vicious torrents with hailstones. Rains are considered blessings in Africa, but then our poor drainage systems and lack of preparedness usually sees them wreaking havoc. None of the organizers had been forward thinking to suggest mitigation procedures in the event of rain, so everyone, including the top management, was caught off guard. With the hailstones falling furiously, everyone sought shelter in the school's dining hall, which was not meant to hold huge numbers at once.

Hundreds of boys and girls squeezed together in the maxed hall creating a perfect environment for mischief. To make the already messed up situation precarious, the thick cloud covering the sky gave the illusion that it was dark, and nothing escalates mischievousness like darkness. Darkness is the proper devil's workshop, coupled with the fact that the mind of an average teenage boy is always on overdrive, especially with girls around. A once organized event sunk into anarchy as cheeky male students took advantage of the situation to grope girls' body parts they only dreamt of.

At some point, the rain subsided and students from other schools slipped out to board their buses back to school. No sooner had everyone else left than only Akili students remained huddled in one dark corner of the hall with no sign of a bus to take us back to school. We looked like a rained-on herd of sheep. After all the fun, the harsh reality started dawning on us that we risked sleeping on the cold dining hall floor of a girls' school. Our minds were suddenly restored back to factory settings, a new sobriety descending upon us. As late as 9:00 p.m., Tusker had still not come for us, and that is when we started thinking of options.

We settled on two options. One was to request to sleep in that hall and leave in the morning using public transport, or beg our hosts to drop us with their bus, which was way smaller than ours. We would have had to squeeze like biscuits in a box. Then someone suggested that we send an emissary to prevail upon the head-girl to talk to her teachers to lend us their bus. Our hope lay in the fact that one of us had outdone himself in cajoling her thus we were in her good books. Although it was a tall order, she gave it a shot, only for us to hear the teacher in charge retort that he remembered Akili boys being called severally on the public address system to board their bus.

Secondly, two of our troupe members were so drunk that they kept hurling obscenities, and no school worth its salt will knowingly take responsibility for drunks from another school. I remember one shouting *"kwendaaaa!"* then his counterpart joined in with, "you are being selfish (hic!) With that matchbox you call a bus, (hic!) Eat it." Our hopes of going home diminished. To further compound our woes was the big question awaiting us back at school: why did the bus leave us behind?

By this time, we were subdued, hopeless, and distraught. We staggered slowly out of the school hall and gathered outside the gate, hoping to catch a public service vehicle that would by some miracle still be operating at that hour. The usually busy Kisumu-Kakamega highway was quiet, dark, and cold.

A few minutes to 2 a.m., we heard Tusker's unmistakable roar, then the cracked round headlights came into view. After the torturous wait, we were being picked. There was a huge sigh of relief as everyone scrambled to get on board.

On the drive back, the tension inside Tusker was heavy, a sharp contrast to the excitement witnessed that morning. It was so quiet that for the first time we noticed our bus did not have a meaningful sound system.

A would-be great day had gone so horribly wrong, ushering everyone back to the realities of boarding school, like the pending class assignments we had skipped due to excitement. Whereas some had taken soft loans from friends to impress girls, who would probably never communicate back, others had borrowed clean outfits that now needed to be washed before return. The biggest worry of all, however, was the punishment awaiting us. Tusker roared back into Akili at 3 a.m., probably the latest a school bus has ever returned students back to school.

BOOKED

"IF YOU LEFT HERE ON Saturday to go represent the school at the drama festivals, step forward."

Those were the opening remarks by Bokassa the following Monday at assembly. It was no surprise because we all knew our actions over the weekend had gone overboard. It was time to pay for the error of our ways. I had finally been caught. Since my first encounter with FS, I had managed to stay clear of trouble. FS had failed to link me to the botched student strike. I may have been problematic but not to the point of being recalcitrant to burn the school. Nothing would have made me to participate in the strike.

"Quick, we do not have the whole day here!" Bokassa shouted.

I joined my colleagues at the front, who were trying

to find the less rugged parts on the ground to kneel on. We knelt that morning from the time Bokassa started his speech, until the assembly was dismissed. Our knees were painful, sore, and numb. Scenes flashbulbed in mind: all the times I had *jomped* without being caught, the evening I checked into school while drunk, the food heist, and the breaking into the administration block to steal SQR's Palito and successfully hiding in plain sight.

The chair I sat on in class was stolen; I had worn a shopped shirt to that festival, and the previous week I had sold cigarettes to get the cash to splurge on at the festival. The litany of misdemeanours had slipped through the fingers of the hawk-eyed administration, but here I was. I had thought that with Atom and Lethal as my friends, my name was immune from the Black Book. I was wrong.

One after the other, we were ushered into the deputy head teacher's office and issued with our suspension letters. There was no chance to explain yourself or apologize. You only walked in, gave your details and stood aside to wait for the secretary to draft your letter. Usually, the school had pre-printed suspension letters on a template, leaving blank spaces for the name, class, reason of suspension, terms and date of return. The slip was run through the typewriter and his details keyed in. I looked at my document:

NAME: Hillary Lisimba

CLASS: Form 3 Red

REASONS FOR SUSPENSION: Causing disturbance at a school outing, and refusing to board the bus back to school.

TERMS OF RETURN: Report back after

two (2) weeks accompanied by at
least one parent and a fine of five
hundred shillings (KShs. 500) for
wasted fuel.
SUSPENSION NUMBER: One.

The bit about suspension number existed to show whether you were a first or multiple offender. Every student was allowed a maximum of two cautions; the third was an expulsion without negotiation. I had blown into my first caution; swiftly getting into the dreaded Black Book. One more punishable offence and my chance at Akili would be hanging in the balance.

As I headed home that morning, I could not account for those hours that had occasioned my suspension. I did nothing with it—no task I undertook, no new girlfriend, no critical life hack. I had gained absolutely nothing but a blot on my record. It would have made more sense to be suspended for *jomping,* because I made money out of it, but this? I had won the battle, but lost the war. The regrets hit home hard. I had allowed myself to get caught up in the euphoria and followed the crowds, like a lemming. Alone, I wouldn't have made such a decision, not in a million years.

Now, the suspension letter had only my name and it was addressed to my parents. When all was done and dusted, you are only responsible for your actions and behaviour; the long arm of the law plucked everyone individually. The thought of facing my parents was chilling. I considered going home, hiding the letter and showing back after two weeks with a parent for hire. I knew there were many men and women of reasonable age around Kiboswa who could be paid to role-play. The problem was actors tend to overdo things to earn their pay, so when the punishment hour came after meeting the disciplinary committee, such 'parents' would clobber you senseless.

Regardless of how annoyed and disappointed with you your real parents are, they punish you with love, strangers feel nothing. The unanswered question was what I would give my parents as the reason for being home for two weeks, less than a month after opening school.

I chose to take responsibility for my action and accept the consequences. *I will give them the letter and wait for their worst.*

Hiring fake parents would have cost me an arm and a leg, money I did not want to spend, as I was still recovering from repaying that pair of shoes my furry friend destroyed. With that decided, another difficult question was whether I would go as early as possible, or linger around somewhere, and then show up in the evening like sheep being shepherded back home from grazing. Going in the morning would have helped me find bearing, face the consequences, and be done with it. The problem of getting home in the morning was that my parents would still be full of energy to scold and beat me more and severely.

In the evening, their minds would be tired and energy levels low. The risk was not being beaten severely that evening, then waking up to another round of beating the following morning. I had never before struggled to make a decision like I did that morning.

Dad was in his shop and Mom at work when I got home. The moment our eyes met, I changed my mind about revealing upfront my reasons for being home. The best bet was to hold onto that bit of information for as long as possible, and if by some miracle no one asked, I would keep it to myself. For the time being, I would enjoy the little luxuries that home offered; but boarding school denied me: television, food, and warm bathing water, I decided.

My holidaying was cut short a few hours later when Mom came back from work. Her first question was why I was home yet my fees had been paid in full. She must have looked at me and ruled out sickness, so she was sure I was not home for medication. Furthermore, the school always made a point of informing parents about a sick student before he was sent home. It was even preferred that the parent picked their son from school.

I avoided her eyes.

"Speak!" she demanded.

"I am home on suspension."

"What?"

"I have been suspended for two weeks."

With that, she walked away without saying anything. Her reaction and silence was the worst torture; I wanted to know what was going through her mind. It is better for someone to erupt immediately so that they let out the anger, otherwise keeping quiet makes it percolate in the mind, and magnify tenfold. She had not even asked what had led to my suspension. The only advantage with the break was that it offered the opportunity to receive the bad news in manageable bits. If I shared news about my suspension, and immediately followed it with the stupid reason behind that shameful incident, she would probably have exploded and rained blows on me.

I was seated on a bench in the patio thinking about my life when ferocious blows landed on my head. It was Dad. From the look of things, Mom had broken the news to him. Mr Ambani did not wait to get the whole story. The moment he heard 'suspended,' he flipped, and he was brutal. I tried to duck or block the blows with my arms, but I did not succeed. By the time he stopped, my eardrums were wheezing as if a mosquito had flown into my ear and was roving in there. My head was pounding and I felt like I was swollen in so much pain that I avoided looking at myself in the mirror. I could feel several lumps on my head, but was not sure I wanted to see how swollen they were.

At dinner that evening, I was ordered to explain in detail the reasons for my suspension. I produced the suspension letter. My parents told me to read word by word aloud so that my younger sisters too would hear, and know how disgraceful their elder brother was. The temperatures in the room rose, the tension so high that even my sisters found it impossible to enjoy their dinner. My old man was enraged; he kept pacing up and down the house in search of something he could not seem to find. Thatcher said little, she just kept her legs propped towards the vents of the room heater.

I wished the suspension had been due to sneaking; it would have offered me the opportunity to use reverse psychology on Mom and blame her for not listening to me when I needed her most to help me stay clear of trouble.

The two weeks dragged. Some days, my parents would invite counsellors and elders to lecture me on the importance of education. I had become the unwanted child in my parents' home; even my sisters associated with me from a distance, for fear of being reprimanded. My actions had strained my relationship with my family so much that I lived like a destitute. No one informed me when food was ready or asked whether I had eaten to my fill. I would peep through my bedroom window to ascertain there was no sign of my parents, sneak into the main house, serve my share and troop back to my hiding.

Things were so tough that I could not cough or sneeze freely, and if I did it had to be discreetly. I hated the chasm that was opening between me and my people, but the further I kept away from them, the better for both of us. Chances were that if we kept meeting I would irk them more, and most probably get a fresh beating.

The harrowing period finally came to an end, and it was time to report back to school. In all the three years of high school, I had never been happy going back to boarding, but at that moment it seemed to be more peaceful in school than at home. Both parents accompanied me, a journey of uncomfortable silence. When we got to the office, I was paraded before the disciplinary committee and my sins were read out. FS added two riders; that I was rude to him on my first day at Akili. Although I was exonerated due to lack of evidence, my name appeared on the list of suspects during the strike. My parents just shook their heads, aghast.

As was the norm with suspension returnees, all members on the committee were asked to flog you, in turns. There were no rules to the number of strokes a teacher would give, so this presented another wonderful opportunity for Mr Ogetto to pacify his vendetta against me. He flogged my buttocks with such passion I hated myself for what led to our beef. A random spectator would have thought it is his reputation I had dragged through mud. My parents too were asked to punish me, giving them the last chance to let out all the negative energy against me. They were asked to pay the fine at the bursar's office, and make two extra copies of the receipt. The original was for them to keep, one copy would go into my file for future reference, while the other was added to the transport department's file for use during auditing.

After playing hide and seek with the law for a while, and

getting away with it, my day in the dock had come. I was now officially a booked student. My conscience stabbed me. I wondered what it must have felt for my parents to appear before the committee over a disciplinary case they had no hand in. I made a mental note to change for the better.

With that suspension having dealt a blow to my contraband business, I ventured into the business of hawking bread at night. There were always students who felt hungry after the canteen was closed. I would buy two full loaves, slice them into four parts and price each piece at fifty cents more. By lights off, all the bread was sold, earning me some profit to live on the next day. It was a challenging business because the aroma of fresh bread was tempting, so several times I nibbled on bread meant for sale until there was none left.

I had started spreading tendons far and wide when FS showed up at my palace one night. The 'courtesy call' was to inform me to stop the bread business; that it was illegal for students to sell food to each other. Someone had snitched on me, and if I stuck to my guns, FS would suspend me again. The sentiments caught me by surprise as this same school offered me commerce lessons bi-weekly, and bread trade was the only legitimate venture I had engaged in at the school. The other was made possible through sneaking and dealing with contraband.

I was not the only one doing business in that school, though. Manywele doubled up as the only known Akili student whose box had packets of razor blade and shaving cream. He did not have a beard that needed constant shaving; as a matter of fact, his chin was smoother than a new-born's bottoms. As part of building capacity and earning a coin, he ingeniously started the business of shaving peers who could not afford barbershops in Kiboswa.

Well, he was not exactly a professional barber. His shave left the client's head with haphazard rows of hair, but in a setup like Akili that was as good as a proper shave. Furthermore, what would you expect from a barber who charges you five shillings per cut, the cost of an *andazi*? That is the origin of his nickname, Manywele, Swahili for hair, a name he shared with his closest friend and village-mate, Dennis, who had joined his trade shortly before being appointed the head prefect.

There was more. Every New Year brought with it new developments, especially with uniform as students would report with an additional pair or shoes to replace the aging ones. Newton 'Gravity' Munangwe had this pullover he had worn since he was a *mono*. The more mileage it acquired the more the yarn disintegrated and hang at the elbows. At first, we wondered why his parents would buy him new shoes, trousers, and shirts but never seen the need to replace the pullover, only to learn that they always did. However, it never made it to school. Gravity had entered into an agreement with a uniform seller in a little town called Majengo where he would alight on his way to school, sell the new pullover at a throw away price, then use the proceeds to top up his pocket money.

As happens with every enterprising society, there is always that one character whose thinking goes overboard, leaving the rest wondering what informed those decisions. Ours hit limits that will probably never be replicated. There was an old neighbour who lived alone on a small compound that was visible when standing beside the tank next to Ruwenzori House. The only earthly possessions to his name were a dilapidated mud hut, a stunted mango tree, and an emaciated indigenous cow with long horns. He was an alcoholic, so on many occasions the cow sat under the mango tree chewing cud until late in the night when he staggered back home.

Lethal had embezzled his fees, and rumours were rife that in the coming weeks, Bokassa would send defaulters home. The walls were caving in for him and he had to cough up money, or his Dad would kill him. He watched the desperate cow for a while and reckoned it was the answer to his problems. He was going to steal and sell it, clear the arrears and get over that hurdle. On this one, even we, his most trusted friends, he kept us in the dark lest we talked him out of the crazy idea.

He executed his idea one evening when the neighbour was out drinking and the rest of us in evening preps. Well, as all robberies go, there is a mistake that the robber makes that gives them away. Lethal was in a blue games kit written Akili High School. When villagers saw a young man pulling a cow around at night, they could tell something was amiss. Two pertinent questions came up. If he was a student, which he most likely was, why was he with a cow when school was in session? Two, if he was a villager, the most unlikely option, why was he dressed in an Akili games kit unless he had stolen it from the school's students' clothes line. Whichever way one looked at it, the boy had lifted something and community policing was uncompromising.

He was taken to the police station where he confessed that he was delivering the stolen cow to a butcher in Kisumu. He was sure that once the cow was slaughtered, there would be no evidence of the theft, but his goose was now cooked. He was found guilty of robbery; his covering up for embezzling school fees, which is a forgivable mistake, pushed him into a felony beyond the school's jurisdiction. Lethal now belonged to the Juvenile Correctional System.

INSTITUTIONALIZED

THE PENTECOSTAL CHURCH WHOSE DOOR I passed every night while *jomping* held an annual convention every August. Youths from other churches converged for a week-long event of praise, worship, and glorifying God. The convention always coincided with holiday tuition for form three and four students, a period where the rules were not as stringent as during normal school sessions. Waking up was at 7a.m., there was no teacher on duty and prefects did not exercise authority given the two sets of students were seniors expected to govern themselves. The school too had fewer students so less noise, minimal disruptions and tranquillity that made learning wonderful.

It was the only period where dubbing food was legal but, ironically so, few did. Add to the feeling of knowing that one set of students were exiting the school in a few months, while the other would become candidates and the mood was ecstatic. As easy as life was, holiday tuition remained an important period on the school calendar since most of what was expected in the final exams was revised during this period. In other words, attending August tuition as a candidate was already a guaranteed grade C and above. The one undoing with humans, especially teenagers, is that once you give them a guilt free pass, they tend to go overboard.

Sneaking out of school was illegal, and holidays were no exception, but rules are made to be broken, right? One student sneaked out and attended *kesha* (vigil praise and worship service) at the church during the convention. He brought the news that in all the events we had been to, we were yet to see one gathering with as many young beautiful women like he had seen at that convention. I guess God always picks some of the best beings and gathers them together for Himself, but then it's natural for a few wolves to sometimes stray into the herd and disorient the sheep. We happened to be the wolves.

The following night, a half of the students left their dormitories and went for *kesha*. The number was so high that the administration was informed the boys had spent the night disturbing girls at what should have been a religious event. There was a memo, in bold, on our notice boards the following morning illegalizing attendance to the event next door, both day and night. The one who said that you can halt an advancing army but not an idea whose time has come, was right. The euphoria in us was unstoppable. Where there were beautiful girls, we were going there, memo or not.

Either someone must have whispered to Bokassa that his memo had been ignored like the 'gh' in eight, or he didn't want to leave anything to chance; he sought help from Kiboswa police post. He requested that cops do a night swoop and lock up students who would defy the order. At an ad hoc assembly that evening, he issued a final warning before leaving for his quarters, but then the excitement had gotten into our heads. According to us, this was just another of his empty threats meant to deter us from enjoying our youth. As soon as he was gone, colleagues changed into T-shirts. In groups of four to six, they left for the cathedral, jumping over the same fence I breached now and then. Clearly, many students knew that weak link.

By 9 p.m., seventy percent of the students on holiday tuition were missing. It was a battle with my conscience on whether or not to join since memories of how things had turned last time I followed the crowds were still fresh. Curiosity got the better of me, and I decided to go peep through the fence without necessarily crossing over. That felt safe as only my eyes and mind would have sneaked out, but my body remained within the school compound. No crime committed. No threat of suspension.

The first part of the *kesha* went on without incident until 10 p.m. when there was a short break for congregants to refresh in readiness for a night of worship and dancing. A few felt they had enjoyed enough for the night and headed back, but then there was the insatiable group that stayed on, hoping to push lady luck to the limits and get away with it. Incidentally, everyone saw a police car drive in and park near the chapel door, but we all dismissed it as routine patrol to maintain law and order and guard God's wonderful people. It was an ominous signal that our hormones on fire blinded us from.

Ten minutes into the second session, two tall men in

black hoods covering their heads walked into the chapel with flashlights directed at people's trousers. They had information that anyone in navy blue was a student. A melee ensued soon as we spotted the first few colleagues being dragged to the Black Mariamu. The difference between making it back to school and spending the night in the cells was how fast you could run and outwit the officers. The plain clothes police officers made it trickier; some fleeing students would run right into the jaws of death. They were caught and bundled into the vehicle, their toes barely touching the ground. The minute I saw what was happening, I took off to save myself from the glaring possibility of an arrest, but then scampered into a group of students returning from the chapel. When in danger, you realize Usain Bolt is not the fastest runner the world has ever had, we just lack the motivation.

When we got near the classroom block, we split in different directions to throw anyone following us off balance, since running together like sheep would have increased our chances of being spotted. Running beside me was Academic Angle, who for once thought quickly and slid under the school bus hoping to take cover until things settled. Who would have thought Tusker's roles included hiding students? I was about to dash across the football field when a spotlight flashed in the distance, prompting me to lie flat on the ground. I decided to crawl through that field on my stomach like a lizard and slip into the dormitory unnoticed.

I had just made it into Kilimanjaro when I heard shouts of "*Mberewere anakam!*" Mberewere was the nickname given to the man who had recently replaced FS as deputy, the latter having been promoted to head teacher in a nearby school. Not wanting to waste time, I jumped into bed and covered myself from head to toe; still in my shoes. I pretended to snore as my ears listened to footsteps in the corridor. They came closer, and in what felt like a nightmare, stopped at my bed.

"Get up, stupid ..." Mberewere shouted as he pulled off the blanket from me.

"Look at you; you are even still in shoes. Who do you think you are fooling? Foolish ..."

His vernacular accent was so strong that his pronunciation was devoid of the letters L, P, and D, so the words came out as 'foorish' and 'stuvit,' which made them sound worse than they meant. I wanted to laugh, but had to look like I was really asleep. That is when a bamboo stick fell on my butt and I had to jump out of bed.

"Stavroom ..." He shouted, motioning me out to join those being corralled towards the staffroom.

I knelt down and pleaded innocence, but my words fell on deaf ears. Once again, I had been blinded by euphoria and now risked my second suspension under a new Sherriff. There were over fifty students sprawled on the ground in front of the administration block. Bokassa was standing beside them with a grey electric cable. That cable made a lethal whip. This one had escalated faster than we envisioned. It is when I joined fellow miscreants that I learnt a roll call was taken while we were away. So no amount of hiding was enough to save whoever was not in the dormitory that evening. My heart went out to Academic Angle, who must have been freezing under that bus, but would still face the wrath; the one time he had seemed to have put his brains to proper use.

Those arrested by the cops spent the night at the police post. According to one arrestee, the charges were 'loitering, touting, and causing disturbance to a religious function'.

The good thing about this brouhaha was that no one was suspended; we were only beaten and 'forgiven,' including those who were brought back from the police cells the following morning. This occurrence may have been a small issue for the rest, but it meant a lot to me. It was a reminder that, for the second time, mob psychology almost pushed me down an abyss.

As it turned out, something more sinister happened that night when everyone's focus was on the convention. We would walk into the news when the dining served us black tea, an unwelcome deviation from the traditional white tea we took every day. Students who have just come from a double lesson of mathematics are edgy and irritable, so something as small as tea without milk has potential to degenerate into unrest. Angry crowds were beginning to form when the principal announced that unknown folks, most probably fellow students, had preyed on the previous night's confusion to milk the school cows. When the cowboy tried milking in the morning, there was nothing, just a few drops here and there. Getting less than a cup of milk from the udders of ten well-fed Friesian cows was not normal, so it was a clear case of fraud.

It is how Bokassa explained that turned our temper into a light moment:

"One of you milked our cows last night. We are investigating and treating this as a serious crime. Mr Deputy, if you find the culprit, send him home to bring both parents and, if possible, the whole clan. We shall want to know who among them bewitched him."

The culprits had chosen the perfect time to strike, aware that the cowshed would be the least of anyone's worries that night. When you think about it, who would ever imagine school boys storming the cowshed at night, of all the places? We started formulating a list of suspects in our minds, especially students from the Nandi community. We were told they were the only ones who could drink raw milk directly from a cow. What our minds could not wrap around was whether they hand-milked into cups, or they had suckled. The latter seemed to suffice, because they did not have much time to milk then drink later. Secondly, where was the evidence? Students did not exactly have many places to hide anything, and the security guards had scoured every corner of the compound for leads in vain. From the look of things, the evidence was already in people's stomachs.

A prime suspect was a slender Form Four boy called Keter. It was even funnier when you imagined him, as tall as he was, under a cow's udder. But then everyone seemed to agree that if evidence somehow managed to put him at the scene of crime, he should not be prosecuted as his body was in dire need of love and nourishment. With dead ends from every corner, the administration did not pursue the issue, but it remained something to always laugh about.

RAISON D'ÊTRE

DURING OUR TIME, STUDENTS MADE career choices while in form three. It was a make or break period for many for it guided the combination of subjects to major in. Those days, the lucrative ones were: teaching, aviation, architecture, engineering, medicine, law, or journalism. Most decisions were as a result of what parents wanted their children to be. Hardly did anyone mention career paths in forensics, software development, or food science. Arts like photography, music, acting, as well as sports, were frowned upon. Too bad that in Africa we believe in the white-collar industry, going to offices in suits and briefcases, the allure that is the epitome of making it in life.

A parent cannot withstand seeing you walking across the streets with a guitar strapped on your back, going for a gig, and consider you employed, even when you are making a million dollars per performance. You could be the most dependable player at a well-paying football club, and sending them good money every month, but they will still ask when you plan to get yourself a job. To them, a son or daughter earning peanuts with business cards titled 'Director' or 'Executive' has an aura of being serious with life than another earning more without business cards, an office, nor title.

You will be told to play football as a hobby, while you look for work because, seriously, who the hell is a central midfielder and what exactly do they do? How will your African father go drinking *busaa* in the village and boast that his son earns a living by making people laugh? When did comedy become a career yet they make each other laugh and speak in tongues every day after drinking, but no one pays them? It is against this backdrop that parents, whose children are into informal employment, keep quiet when the rest brag about theirs being doctors and lawyers. They are safer not embarrassing themselves, since the cows they gave birth to are wasting their lives on stupid things.

One area the now defunct 8-4-4 education system failed terribly was that no one taught us the basics of entrepreneurship, management, or sourcing for funding. Not even one chapter in the whole curriculum touched on the aspects of pitching for projects, writing business plans, or networking to look for business partners. In other words, we were drilled to be perennial employees, but not entrepreneurs. Our minds were filled with details on how to write letters seeking employment, how to behave in the office, and manage salaries. Business education was divided into commerce, accounting and economics, most of which was theory, figures and graphs in that order, but nothing practical.

The climax of subject choice would be at Career Day, where parents and teachers sat with students to guide them on courses and universities to select. It is on this day that I had an ugly encounter with Dad. First of all, we loved it when our mothers or sisters visited, because they took the trouble of cooking and bringing food, regardless of how heavy it was. So, when one of the boys informed me that Dad was at the bench waiting, my expectations dimmed. History had shown that whenever he visited, he would bring the day's newspaper, then spend the hours lecturing me about my performance. There was no shopping or food, not even a packet of crisps. His visits were gangster like that.

In the months leading to this big day, I had found my mind, body and soul gravitating full force towards languages and I swallowed them hook, line, and sinker. I became a regular parrot at the interclass debates, avid contributor to the school magazine, and had risen to be Journalism Club chairperson. This can be attributed to two men: the late Mr 'Chaps' Oyoo and Mr Masinde, both teachers of English. Their review of set-books planted in me the seeds of being an author, building on the love for languages I already had from primary school. I desired to be a bestselling author. To put pen to paper and churn out masterpieces that could be read and enjoyed by lovers of literature.

I started reading set books with a purpose, not just to pass exams, but also unravel what was going through the minds of the writers when they weaved those pieces. My *Aha* moment was here, the *raison d'être*. Things had never been that clear to me before. What I did not know was that while I was charting a career path to align with my love for languages, my old man had been researching on what

I needed to secure an admission into the Kenya School of Surveying and Mapping (KISM).

It is at that Career Day that I learnt Dad always wanted me to be a land surveyor, which meant taking Geography as one of the subjects. This was a subject taught by someone I struggled to get along with since form one. I refused to sign the documents from KISM Dad had come with. I wanted to be in the media, and I was not backing down. Backed by one of the teachers, the two prevailed upon me to change my mind on the basis of being older; that they knew where the world was going. Dad reminded me that one of his elder brothers was a surveyor, who was moneyed because of that discipline. I did not want money, I wanted what my heart loved, so I remained resolute about it. My old man was so enraged that he walked out in protest without leaving me what I was most interested in—pocket money.

The confrontation continued when I went home over the holidays to a point of him telling me that journalists are people who are *chap chap*, a quality he was not sure I possessed. I still stood my ground, unless he wanted me to call it a day after high school and start riding a *bodaboda* around Vihiga. He obliged, albeit unwillingly, but I am glad I stuck to my guns. I am one of the very few products of our class who ended up in the career chosen on that day. Many made harried decisions based on the need to impress their parents, or select easier subject combinations, and then got confused when it was time to join university.

What looked like a simple case of parents imposing things on their children, from toys to career paths, altered many young destinies.

DEADLY SLUMBER

Morning Preps, Christened *Chilly*, Was compulsory for senior students. The official time was from 4 a.m. to 6 a.m., essentially forcing us to wake up at 3.30 a.m. in order to be in class on time. The administration took it so seriously that sometimes they fixed early morning exams to send the message that it was part of the school programme. Other times they took roll call and punished latecomers. Apparently, according to Akili, early mornings were the best to study because the mind was fresh.

The struggle served as a push for one to work hard knowing the suffering was just for a season. Truth is that half the time we dozed off, save for the few who had the will power to remain awake by studying with their legs inside a water trough. It was common to watch your desk mate's eyes blink in quick succession, followed by his head tilting to one side, then eyes shutting before he hit his forehead on the locker and was jolted back to life. The process would repeat until the breakfast bell sounded.

Some teachers on duty tiptoed around the classrooms looking to catch those dozing. This called for cohorts with desk mates so that one person slept for the first hour while the other kept watch, then the roles would change in the second hour. The risk was having an imbecile desk mate who would doze off too instead of keeping watch, leaving both of you vulnerable. My desk mate, Symo, was one such character. Half the time, we would both be caught dead asleep when it was his turn to guard. Other times he remained awake, but for some reason failed to catch the sound of approaching footsteps. What he never seemed to notice was that because of his condition, most teachers avoided punishing him lest he undressed and wandered around the school naked, so every time we got caught, I suffered alone.

Now, Bokassa loathed with passion students who dozed off during morning preps. Whenever I remember how hard he slapped me on the face the one day he caught me, I feel like locking myself in a room and crying. And, it did not end there since he still announced it during the assembly.

"This morning I found a young man called Lisimba sleeping in class. A whole Form Three. Records show he scored a D in mathematics last term, and that is the only subject you are allowed to copy, from the log table. Look at him ..."

From that day, every time I said anything to a junior student, they reminded me to use that time on improving my mathematics. Bokassa, the bastion of academic excellence, had reason to talk the way he did though.

He was the only teacher who, according to me, made arithmetic look easy even for us, whose DNA did not mix with numbers. The problem was that being the head of the school, he was always on the move and in meetings, so he hardly got time to handle lessons. The few lessons he taught me during holiday tuition made such a great difference to my overall performance. He was like that super sub player who is brought in when the team seems to have run out of ideas and needs a game changer.

The bad thing about being a teenager is that some habits refuse to go, unless you get killed. Oversleeping and skiving *chilly* was such for me. I would be caught up in another swoop not long after Bokassa's incident. July is one of the coldest months of the year, which meant that in second term, Akili was characterized by long durations of low temperatures. Now, nothing goes hand in hand as perfectly as sleep and the cold, especially in the wee hours of dawn. The temptation to skip morning preps around this period was like a drug. It was even more enticing on Mondays, as the mind struggled to shake out of the weekend hang ups.

One Monday morning, prohibitive weather coincided with bad judgment and every Form Three Red student except Dan skipped *chilly*. That was also the morning Bokassa decided to walk around. He found out that only one student was taking morning preps seriously in our class. What annoyed him even more was that there was an impressive number of form ones in class, yet *chilly* for them was elective. I have never understood why those *monos* were up at 4 a.m., yet all they learnt were definitions of terms.

When I was in form one, all I needed to do was come up with and cram mnemonics, like DRAHOHEROHS for Dryopithecus, Ramapithecus, Homo Habilis, Homo

Erectus, Rhodesian Man to Homo Sapiens. Those *monos* made us look like a class of jokers who were headed towards giving the school bad grades and dragging the overall score through mud.

"I am a worried man because I already know where next year's Ds will come from," Bokassa started during assembly. "And in my grade count an A means you are Alive. B is for Breathing; C you are in a Coma."

Everyone burst out laughing.

"Do not laugh, for that should tell you that D and E stand for Dead and Extinct respectively. That is what Form Three R is working very hard towards: Death."

Every teacher turned to look at Mr Masinga, our class teacher and biology guru. They were searching for his expression as his class was being painted in such negative light by the man at the helm. He was nonchalant, but most of us knew that the anger boiling inside him was hot enough to boil crocodile meat. In form one when he was appointed our class teacher, he told us to try not to step on his toes because, although they were rare, his whips were close to imprisonment. Now, a whole class had jumped up and down on his toes like youngsters on a bouncing castle. That was not the kind of teacher to annoy as he was poor at anger management.

We had not even settled in class when Mr Masinga walked in carrying a bundle of bamboo sticks. You need to have been caned with a bamboo to know the magnitude of pain it inflicts, and it does not break into pieces like normal tree branches.

"Homo Sapiens!"

That was how he always referred to us. There was no answer, everyone was quivering.

"HOMO SAPIENS!" He repeated, banging the table top

with a clenched fist.

"Yes, Sir."

"I will not have the principal single out my class during assembly over students I have brought up so well."

This was by all means laughable, as most of us were crooks masquerading as good boys, only that some had been lucky enough to avoid capture. But hey, if our class teacher's prima facie belief was that his boys were so wonderful, who were we to deny? He may have said the words calmly, but you could tell that deep within he was he was trying hard to suppress the anger, and it continued to seethe as he spoke. His eyes roved over the whole class, and I bet we could see the heart palpitating by the way the left side of his chest throbbed.

"I have tried to give you space. Brought you up as responsible adults who can run things maturely, but no, you still want me to boss you around like form ones."

Goodness gracious, he was holding back tears. It was evident he wanted to scream his lungs out, but he held back. It was the first time I was seeing him look frustrated. Mr Masinga always seemed to have things under control; an alpha male, I bet because he knew his extremes were gory. An excruciating pain pierced through my chest, stabbing right into my heart's left ventricle. I could swear this was severe pneumonia, or my pulmonary artery was sending too much de-oxygenated blood to the lungs, and I was trembling.

"If you missed morning preps today, and you do not have a letter from the nurse to show you were sick, stand up."

He moved to the window and stared into space, giving us time to stand up. We got up sluggishly, still shaking.

"I am going to give ten to each civilian and fifteen to all

the prefects, understood?"

No one answered. We were too traumatized to even nod our heads, let alone say anything.

Mr Masinga flogged us that morning to a point our class prefect pulled out his red tie and announced he was resigning from leadership. I can tell you that no one tastes power in Akili then voluntarily gives it up. After the lashing, we were tasked with uprooting a huge tree stump, and splicing it into smaller chunks for use as firewood in the kitchen. The school was proud to own three axes that were blunt, so only three of us would be working at a time, the pace painstakingly slow. The rest offered moral support in the form of jokes and stories.

The punishment created a collegial bond since for the first time, civilians and prefects had the same punishment, and with everyone working towards a common goal. The punishment dragged on for two long weeks, leaving us with blistered hands.

LAST MILE

FORM FOUR RED IS THE last classroom at the end of the long U-shaped structure that is the Akili classrooms. From the entrance, it is the first classroom that comes into view as you walk in. The location affords it a vantage three-dimensional view of Akili's topography. Through the windows on the right side you can see the stretch of murram road that snakes out to the main gate, a view that gave us foresight into the day we would trudge that path after bidding farewell to Akili. For the time being, it helped us observe visitors and teachers as they walked in and out of the school.

The windows on the left side opened to the vast space in front of the classrooms block; a convergence point for everything that happened from other classes. The third was through the door, giving a wide view of the huge administration block straight ahead with the Kenyan flag towering above on a white metallic pole. Further ahead you could also see a section of the football field and an obstructed view of the dormitories.

Outside the classroom, an enormous round concrete tank sits at the front right corner like a sentinel. It is the largest thus the school's last reservoir of hope during the dry season. The moment Tank 4R poured out its last gush of water, everyone knew the school was in trouble. By virtue of it being next to our classroom, we, the seniors, figured we kind of owned it, hence lobbied for one set of keys. It was a diplomatic approach to a bigger plan; one the administration should have just listened to and saved everyone a lot of trouble. But does the administration ever listen?

Manywele, in his wisdom, believed that form fours were too senior to fight over water with juniors, who still had several years at Akili. Moreover, as candidates, we needed more time in class to study and make the school proud, which made sense to take over to the administration. We could bring our odds and ends to class, and then do our cleaning behind the block during evening preps. If you look at the issue from our point of view, it was futuristic, because it would ease competition at water points, the school would have clean candidates, and our time would be channelled into revision. Dormitories would only be for sleeping.

When the administration rejected our proposal, a dubious approach kicked in, thanks to the school having drilled us into believing that what needs to be done has to be done, by hook or crook. We devised a way of siphoning water out of Tank 4R through the overflow vent at the top, and showering at night behind our classroom. It started with four students then six, then ten, soon the whole class would be waiting for the cover of darkness to squat on the grass and shower on stolen water. Nevertheless, with high school vices, if you don't stop as early as when you can, they become habits to a delusion of legality. We grew so bold that some students forgot it was wrong, and began showering in broad daylight.

One fine evening, at about 8.30 p.m., we gathered at the usual spot, siphoned water out and lined up a meter from each other for our shower. Madam Blue, who was on duty that week, had decided to do a final walk-around to confirm everything was in order before retreating to her quarters. She was unaware that one part of that compound was a community bathroom, so when she heard the sound of water pouring, curiosity led her to investigate. That must have been one of the most shocking scenes she had ever bumped into in her teaching career. In the darkness, her eyes adjusted to silhouettes of boys kneeling beside their troughs scooping and throwing water onto their bodies. One of the silhouettes was mine. Blue stood rooted where she was, like Lot's wife's pillar of salt, and stared at us.

We goggled back through silence that seemed to scream 'what next?' each of us waiting for the other to make the next move. Thankfully, she could not mark out our faces. In her prudence, she dashed to the staffroom and came back with male teachers as backup to apprehend us. It looked like a good idea on paper, but what she forgot was that we were just naked; not rooted there, and definitely not stupid. We quickly poured the water away and threw the troughs across the fence. After that, we shook our bodies vigorously to dry, dressed up and settled back in class, heads buried in books.

When the two came back there was no one, and the

only evidence was the soggy ground. Where does one start finding the culprits when everyone was now busy reading? With no suspects to castigate, we were given a collective 'shame on you' proclamation during assembly the following morning.

With what became known as the *Ndethe Scandal* behind us, we embarked on another equally stupid project—planning the academic fire. This was an illegal bonfire behind the dormitories on the eve of the last paper of the form four final exams. It was frowned upon by the administration, loathed by Bokassa, but loved beyond measure by final-year students. It was a rite of passage, transitioning from a teenager to an adult; therefore, all the books that were associated with that stage needed to be reduced to ashes, the smoke carrying into the sky all the bad memories. The academic fire brought the feeling of breaking away from the chains of bondage. It was like watching the Biblical Israelites walking on the other side of the Red Sea after witnessing an army of Egyptian soldiers drown behind them.

A crowd gathered around the blaze singing war songs, the numbers increasing as more books flew into the raging flame. Finishing high school was war hence the genre of music. The four years in that environment is war against a harsh regime, colleagues, own conscience, and students in other schools across the country. Like prisoners, who were ready to re-join the society after serving their time, or being granted presidential pardon, we were leaving behind history, but the future was a blank slate. Tomorrow was waiting for each one of us to make a mark, and either move to the next level or fade out into oblivion.

At some point, there were no more books to add, and the crowd slowly tapered the same way it had grown.

Every candidate would sleep that night with a feeling of a conqueror, that after bending rules, breaking some, going hungry and surviving the teachers' disciplinary measures, they had made it to the homestretch in one piece. A considerable number of students fall by the wayside through expulsion, death, transfers, dropping out, or were sieved at form three after failing to meet the threshold.

I watched the last strand of smoke slither lazily above the mound of ash in sinuous rings. A light breeze blew, dissipating the last traces of my life in Akili. It was time to go back to my dormitory and think about my final paper the next day. That was it, the proverbial last nail in the coffin. People who had sat as desk mates for years would lose touch after the last exam, and probably never meet again.

For some, they would learn from their teenage mistakes and get a new lease of life and others who would forever carry the scars, both physical and emotional, like Lethal. He sat his final exams while in juvenile detention. A police car dropped him on exam day accompanied by two cops; he was sequestered in one room with his left hand cuffed to a desk until he was done. After that, they returned him to detention until the following day. Despite the conditions, he managed to score an impressive C. He finished his lockup, joined a university and graduated with a Degree in Business Administration. However, that prison stamp on his profile locked him out of many wonderful opportunities, because in Kenya, for you to secure an employment, employers ask for a Certificate of Good Conduct, and getting one when your fingerprints are in the police database is a never-ending nightmare.

Back to the dormitory, I walked into a scene where a mono, Felix, knelt down surrounded by a group of students next to my palace. I gouged out a chunk of his mattress, sprinkled water on it, and used it to wipe my shoes as I watched him being heckled. According to sources, Felix had been eyeing the position of class prefect since the year started, so he initiated several projects to build a reputation. Half of them were not adopted, because like any African politician, his ideas were at sixes and sevens.

However, there was one that was embraced by all: buying a padlock so that their classroom would be locked every time they went out. This was to protect their valuables from being stolen by seniors. The proposal was simple and straightforward—every student contributes five shillings, Felix buys a padlock and latch on the next free walk, then a replica key would be given to one representative from each row. Having lost desks and seats before, the form ones quickly bought into the idea, and Felix collected in excess of one hundred and fifty shillings.

However, the money-loving devil paid him a visit, he ran out of pocket money before the next free walk, and used the money his class had contributed. With the fear for whistling overwhelming his integrity, he started embezzling the money five shillings at a time. Before Felix knew it, there was no money or padlock. The class started pressuring him for their money, and one day he snapped and threatened to bite whoever asked him about the money again, securing him a sitting with the guidance and counselling master. With his classmates broke, they stormed his palace and demanded a way forward, and when their money would be reimbursed.

That failed padlock project cost Felix his peace as well as chances of being a prefect; someone else was handed the baton the day Bokassa announced the new team of leaders. Then again, no right-thinking administration can vest

Hillary Lisimba Ambani

power in a student who threatens to bite his peers because they sought accountability.

Φ

EPILOGUE

Biology Paper 3, A Practical exam, was my final paper. We stepped into the laboratory and the first specimen on the dissecting table was a fish, something we had revised a week before the exam. Either Mr Masinga had stumbled on leakage that showed this question would come, or it was all serendipity. At that point, pain from that flogging he had given us the previous year for oversleeping evaporated into thin air, and he became the day's hero. You just needed to look at the expressions on everyone's face to know who was sure of the first ten marks, and who was regretting not taking the revision seriously.

The lesson I picked on this day was that it is easy to forgive; you just need to pull one heroic or kind act at the hour of need, and all your sins are forgotten. It gave me an insight into why we perennially vote for bad leaders, complain about bad governance for the whole period, then vote them back again after a few promises. Mr Masinga would easily have been overwhelmingly voted into power that day if such a thing happened, including a vote from that prefect he beat to resignation.

I walked majestically from the laboratory with my cardboard, looking with nostalgia at the paths I had trudged for years. All that had come to an end. I had gathered hands-on experience to help me face the world; most of it through a baptism of fire. The struggles, evenings in the library, queues for food, punishments, et al. All that was now history. I had learnt how to respect authority and adjust to different regimes, now it was time to say goodbye to a place I had called home for four years.

The Duke of Vihiga was now a sage. I felt like a soldier from war, and now I was boarding Transall C-160 back home. For the first time, it hit me that I had gotten used to the place so much that the thought of leaving gave me a hollow feeling. Every minute that went by drew me closer to being a villager, or what Bokassa called a squatter.

After years of mischief with my gang, Atom and I had scrapped through to the end with one suspension each, not forgetting the close shaves. As a matter of fact, the two of us had made it this far because we toned down on our mischief when Lethal was thrown into juvenile. Seeing him sit exams while guarded by warders was even more traumatizing for us. Chances are that if he had shared his plan earlier, we would have joined him in stealing that cow, and ended up where he was.

The suspension made me stop *jomping* with wanton disregard for the law, and my grades picked up again. Atom, on the other hand, stopped dubbing and directed to revision the time he wasted on plotting how to go back to the food window. On our last night at Akili, he confided in me that he decided to let go of the nasty grudge he had held against the school head boy. "Jacob has slapped me so painfully today; the day we meet at a secluded corner, I will kill him," he told me the day the head student got on his hit list. I was glad he had found it in his heart to forgive his nemesis, let bygones be bygones, and freed his mind from the choking venom.

As for Academic Angle, I really hoped that he for once did justice to his nickname by performing better in their end year exams to move a step ahead. That hamster wheel was not doing him any good.

ACKNOWLEDGEMENTS

For this wonderful memoir, I owe it to:

Brenda Oloo and Milan Crispo, the two who perennially impact my creative process with a touch of boundless love, magic, and understanding.

Mom, Anne, Julliet, Anto, as well as the late Mr Ambani and Nelly Eboso. Nothing is as wonderful in life as family.

The Akili Boys' High School fraternity, for the years of unforgettable moments, lessons, love, and hate. Special mention to one Michel Otieka, who in his manifold wisdom helped write 'The Poisoned Chalice' chapter.

Vincent de Paul, who always gives life to my words, Mary Koech, my editor, as well as Lydiah Njuguna, Patricia George, and Cassandra Mathews, who keep believing in me to do this.

My lovely fans and readers. It is your undying love and presence that has kept this flame burning.

The Almighty God, who pours thoughts, energies, and new life into my heart each new day. Without Him all this would be vanity.

ABOUT THE AUTHOR

Hillary Lisimba is a TV Producer; he has worked for *Grapevine* and *Taj Show* on Kenya Broadcasting Corporation (KBC), as well as other corporate productions across the borders. *Ministry of Misdemeanor* is his second book, a sequel to *The Boy with Shoes*. He writes *Daddy Diaries*, a weekly column in the *Daily Nation* newspaper. He is also a contributor for *Sauti ya Afrika*, a quarterly African magazine published in the Netherlands. Away from the media and writing, he runs a philanthropic initiative called 'Project Handover' which distributes books and stationery to children's homes across the country. He was a speaker at Safaricom's Engage, Edition 23, dubbed *My Life, My Wife, and Kilimani Moms*.